Some Small Countries Do It Better

Some Small Countries Do It Better

Rapid Growth and Its Causes in Singapore, Finland, and Ireland

Shahid Yusuf

Kaoru Nabeshima

THE WORLD BANK
Washington, D.C.

ISBN (paper): 978-0-8213-8846-4
ISBN (electronic): 978-0-8213-8925-6
DOI: 10.1596/978-0-8213-8846-4

Library of Congress Cataloging-in-Publication Data has been requested.

Cover design: Richard Fletcher, Fletcher Design.
Cover photos: Singapore–Design Pics/thinkstock.com; Finland–Harryfn/Dreamstime.com; Ireland–Selensergen/istockphoto.com.

Contents

Tables

Preface and Acknowledgments

This book is an outcome of a series of study visits to Singapore for African policy makers initiated by Jee-Peng Tan in 2005 with support from Tommy Koh in Singapore and Birger Fredriksen, Yaw Ansu, and Dzingai Mutumbuka at the World Bank. The idea of writing a comparative study of three small economies germinated following a third visit in which the authors participated in discussions with Jee-Peng, who encouraged the authors to explore the contribution of institutions and human capital to the successful performance of small economies and to draw lessons from this experience for late-starting African economies, and who championed the preparation of a study. Vital encouragement and support was also forthcoming from Obiageli Ezekwesli, Vice President of the Africa Region; Ritva Reinikka, Sector Director, Human Development, Africa Region; and Raj Nallari at the World Bank Institute. Typically the gestation period for books, even fairly slender ones, can be long, and in the eighteen months during which we intermittently worked on the manuscript, we accumulated many debts: to our reviewers—Linda English, Vikram Nehru, Ismail Ridwan, Jorma Routti, and Michel Welmond—who offered numerous penetrating comments and suggestions that improved both content and presentation; and to our loyal and hard-working researchers, Rory Birmingham and Lopamudra Chakraborti. Many others indirectly contributed through their backing for the study visits and the project. These include Koh Tin Fook, former Director of the Technical Cooperation Directorate at the Ministry of Foreign Affairs in Singapore; Lee Sing Kong, Director of the National Institute of Education; Law Song Seng, former Director and CEO of the Institute of Education; Chan Lee Mun, Principal of the Nanyang Polytechnic; and Jayakrishnan Gopalakrishnan, Director of the International Operations (Americas) Group at International Enterprise Singapore. Last but not least, we owe thanks to the governments of Norway and Singapore, which financed the project and through it, the background research, the writing, and the publication of this book.

About the Authors

Shahid Yusuf is currently Chief Economist of The Growth Dialogue at the George Washington University School of Business in Washington, DC. He holds a PhD in economics from Harvard University, and a BA in economics from Cambridge University. Prior to joining The Growth Dialogue, Dr. Yusuf was on the staff of the World Bank. During his 35-year tenure at the World Bank, Dr. Yusuf was the team leader for the World Bank–Japan project on East Asia's Future Economy from 2000–09. He was the Director of the *World Development Report 1999/2000, Entering the 21st Century*. Prior to that, he was Economic Adviser to the Senior Vice President and Chief Economist (1997–98), Lead Economist for the East Africa Department (1995–97), and Lead Economist for the China and Mongolia Department (1989–93).

Dr. Yusuf has written extensively on development issues, with a special focus on East Asia, and has also published widely in various academic journals. He has authored or edited 24 books, some of which have been translated into multiple languages, on industrial and urban development, innovation systems, and tertiary education. His five most recent books are *Development Economics through the Decades* (2009); *Tiger Economies under Threat* (co-authored with Kaoru Nabeshima, 2009); *Two Dragonheads: Contrasting Development Paths for Beijing and Shanghai* (co-authored with Kaoru Nabeshima, 2010); *Changing the Industrial Geography in Asia: The Impact of China and India* (co-authored with Kaoru Nabeshima, 2010); and *China Urbanizes* (co-edited with Tony Saich, 2008). Dr. Yusuf lives in Washington, DC, and also consults with the World Bank and with other organizations.

Kaoru Nabeshima is Director, Technological Innovation and Economic Growth Studies Group, Institute of Developing Economies–Japan External Trade Organization (IDE-JETRO), holds a PhD in economics from University of California-Davis, and a BA in economics from Ohio Wesleyan University. Prior to joining IDE-JETRO in 2010, he was a staff member and consultant to the World Bank. During his tenure at the World Bank, which began in 2001, he was a team member for the World Bank–Japan project on East Asia's Future Economy. His recent publications include *Tiger Economies under Threat* (co-authored with Shahid Yusuf, 2009); *Two Dragonheads: Contrasting Development Paths for Beijing and Shanghai* (co-authored with Shahid Yusuf, 2010); and *Changing the Industrial Geography in Asia: The Impact of China and India* (co-authored with Shahid Yusuf, 2010). His research interests lie in East Asia's economic development, especially in the innovation capabilities of firms.

Abbreviations

A*STAR	Agency for Science, Technology, and Research (Singapore)
EDB	Economic Development Board (Singapore)
EEC	European Economic Community
EU	European Union
FDI	foreign direct investment
GATT	General Agreement on Tariffs and Trade
GDP	gross domestic product
GPT	general-purpose technology
GSM	Global System for Mobile Communications
ICT	information and communication technology
IDA	Industrial Development Agency (Ireland)
I-O	input-output
IT	information technology
ITE	Institute of Technical Education (Singapore)
LIS	learning and innovation system
MNC	multinational corporation
OECD	Organisation for Economic Co-operation and Development
PAP	People's Action Party
PISA	Programme for International Student Assessment
R&D	research and development
Sifire	Singapore, Finland, and Ireland
Sitra	Finnish Innovation Fund
SMEs	small and medium-size enterprises
STEM	science, technology, engineering, and mathematics
Tekes	Funding Agency for Technology and Innovation (Finland)
TEU	20-foot equivalent unit
TFP	total factor productivity
TIMSS	Trends in International Mathematics and Science Study
USPTO	U.S. Patent and Trademark Office

1

Looking for Growth

Economic growth is an endlessly fascinating and seemingly inexhaustible topic. Experience and research are steadily enlarging our knowledge, and one needs only to glance at papers written a couple of decades ago to appreciate the great strides in analytic sophistication and empirical verification. Starting in the 1960s—earlier if Japan is included—a number of East Asian economies began achieving growth rates well above the average and were able to maintain that pace until nearly the end of the 1990s. The first set of "flying geese"[1]—the Republic of Korea; Hong Kong SAR, China; Singapore; and Taiwan, China—followed in the wake of Japan, the pacesetter and exemplar. They were joined by Malaysia and Thailand in the 1970s and by Indonesia in the 1980s. The collective growth experience of these economies, which has been exhaustively examined and variously interpreted, serves as the compass for countries aspiring to a higher level of economic performance. But this deepening knowledge, impressive though it is, has yet to produce the robust and broadly applicable policy formulas that practitioners of development are seeking. Almost every country in the world is struggling to raise potential growth rates and to squeeze a few additional percentage points—or even a single additional percentage point—of growth from investment in productive assets; however, even a broadly coordinated application of tested policies cannot guarantee success, and few countries can manage a coordinated application and systematic implementation of policies. They must be content with *second-best* approaches and *policy satisficing.*

---

[1] The term *flying geese* was introduced by Akamatsu in the 1930s and was later presented in a paper published in English (Akamatsu 1962).

In the majority of cases, growth outcomes of late starters have fallen short of expectations.[2] Developed economies averaged growth rates of 2.4 percent between 1990 and 2008, and Germany and Japan averaged rates of 1.9 and 1.5 percent, respectively. Developing economies have collectively increased their gross domestic product (GDP) by an average of 4.7 percent per year over the same period.[3] A small number of emerging economies notched up growth rates of 7 percent per year for a period of 25 years or more,[4] but the majority of these economies have experienced a trend deceleration since 1997 to 1998, leaving only three economies with growth rates exceeding 7 percent per year between 2000 and 2008: China (10.0 percent), India (7.1 percent), and Vietnam (7.5 percent).

Countries, large and small, have struggled to imitate the industrial prowess of the East Asian pacesetters and to exploit the opportunities presented by globalization to expand exports. But approximating the East Asian benchmarks has proven difficult, and growth accelerations have tended to be remarkably transient.[5] Building a portfolio of tradable goods and services and steadily raising the level of investment in these activities have generally defied the best policy efforts. (In particular, bringing investment ratios on par with East Asian averages has presented the greatest challenge.) Thus, for most countries, the East Asian model has remained a stretch. Growing at high single-digit rates, as the East Asian economies did and some still do, demands GDP investment ratios of 30 percent or more. Hence, the search is on for growth recipes not so tightly bound to investment, to manufacturing activities, and to the export of manufactured products.[6]

---

[2]Growth accelerations have for the most part been short lived, with a strong tendency for countries to revert to a global mean rate of growth (see Durlauf, Johnson, and Temple 2004; Yusuf 2009). Easterly (2009, 7), relying on the findings of panel regressions of annual growth rates, observes that "only 8 percent of the variance is permanent cross-country differences, the other 92 percent is transitory deviations . . . from a world mean of 1.8 percent per capita annual increase."

[3]Per capita growth rates in the poorer countries are much lower because populations have been expanding. Once resource depletion and environmental externalities are factored in, the growth achievements to date are further diminished.

[4]The elite 13—Botswana; Brazil; China; Hong Kong SAR, China; Indonesia; Japan; Korea; Malaysia; Malta; Oman; Singapore; Taiwan, China; and Thailand—were justly celebrated in the report issued by the Commission for Growth and Development (2008).

[5]For more about growth accelerations, see the article by Hausmann, Pritchett, and Rodrik (2005) and the subsequent reappraisal and critique of their findings by Xu (2011) using an augmented data set.

[6]Several of the fast-growing economies also benefited from an abundance of natural resources and the export of resource-intensive products. The economic successes of countries such as Botswana, Indonesia, and Malaysia, for example, are closely linked to the exploitation of energy, land, and mineral resources.

In casting around for recipes of this type that are validated by demonstrated results, one is drawn to the experience of economies that relied less on the sheer volume of capital spending (or an abundance of natural resources) and more on other drivers of growth: human capital and knowledge. Finland and Ireland are among the tiny band of nations that grew rapidly for well over a decade by adopting an approach that derived the maximum mileage from an adequate investment in physical assets and by harnessing the potential of human capital and technologies. Singapore adopted a hybrid approach that embraces the high investment, export-led East Asian model, but by quickly moving to build its human and knowledge assets, the country was able to diversify much faster into higher-technology manufactures and tradable services than some of the other East Asian economies. Such diversification allowed Singapore to maintain higher growth rates over a longer period.[7]

The path followed by these three countries offers a different perspective on growth. Their approach may be of greater relevance than the well-worn East Asian model in the highly competitive global environment of the early 21st century because it does not necessarily assume heroic levels of investment. Moreover, it may be better tailored to the opportunities available to a heterogeneous group of middle- and lower-middle-income economies aiming for growth rates in the 6 percent range, as well as to late-starting, low-income countries that, because of their youthful, rapidly increasing populations, need to grow at high single-digit rates to create enough jobs and to double per capita income in 10 years.

Efforts to accelerate growth and sustain higher trend rates—by late starters as well as middle-income economies—must be tempered by three considerations.[8] First, resource scarcities, rising energy prices, environmental pressures, and the

---

[7]The three countries followed a course defined by the Arrow–Lucas–Romer model of endogenous growth.

[8]The question posed by David Landes (1990)—"Why are we so rich and they so poor?"—remains unanswered. Neither the neoclassical growth models nor the more recent models of endogenous growth have convincingly explained the divergence between incomes and levels of development across the world or why for many poor countries backwardness has not served as a springboard to faster growth. As Robert Solow (2007, 5–6) observed, "Some of the literature gives the impression that it is after all pretty easy to increase the long-run growth rate. Just reduce a tax on capital here or eliminate an inefficient regulation there, and the reward is fabulous, a higher growth rate forever. . . . But in real life it is very hard to move the permanent growth rate; and when it happens, as perhaps in the USA in the later 1990s, the source can be a bit mysterious even after the fact." The literature on the investment climate also creates the impression that higher growth rates can be achieved if countries can muster the political will to engage in institutional regulatory reforms so as to reduce a number of transaction costs, lower factor market impediments, and ease infrastructure bottlenecks that weigh on businesses. See for example the comparison of business climates in China and India by Li, Mengistae, and Xu (2011).

maturing of globalization[9] are undermining policy-induced growth impulses. Second, the economies of the European Union (EU) and the United States, which served as sources of demand in the recent past, face strong headwinds that are largely of their own creation[10] but are undoubtedly problematic for late-starting countries that must export to accelerate growth. Third, development economics is faced with a policy deficit.[11] The advances in theory and the deepening of empirical analysis have yielded only a meager crop of ideas on how countries can realize development goals, and the effective implementation of better policies is needed for countries to realize their growth ambitions.[12] The East Asian model has served as the policy workhorse for decades. Supplementing it with other models is a matter of urgency.

This chapter starts with a brief review of the sources of growth and moves quickly to identify factors that could contribute to growth through higher productivity, thereby increasing the range of policy interventions and models that could be put to the test in developing countries. African countries figure prominently in this group, and they are among the ones most urgently searching for ways to accelerate growth, either by building manufacturing capacity and generating demand through exports much like the East Asian Tigers or by creatively using hybrid approaches based on a range of activities, with human capital and technology serving as the principal drivers.[13]

As is apparent from table 1.1, Sub-Saharan economies have picked up speed[14] and pulled ahead of the average growth rate for the world (but not the average for low-income countries), but their per capita GDP growth rates remain the lowest, their per capita incomes are a fraction of global per capita GDP, and their share of global product is only 1.4 percent (tables 1.2 and 1.3).

---

[9]See Ghemawat (2011), Hufbauer and Suominen (2010), James (2009), and Rodrik (2011) for recent views on the state of globalization and its future.

[10]Import demand from the EU and the United States is likely to be weaker for some time. As several EU economies and the United States struggle to rectify domestic and external resource imbalances, they could be less prolific sources of innovation, and the offshoring of industry and of tradable impersonal services may slow. Over the longer term, aging and declining populations will be a brake on growth.

[11]On the policy lessons from growth economics, see Aghion and Durlauf (2009) and Yusuf (2009). On the contribution of aid to growth performance, see Doucouliagos and Paldam (2009).

[12]See Pritchett, Woolcock, and Andrews (2010) on policy implementation failures.

[13]Recently, some effort has gone into encapsulating the Chinese and Indian models of development. But codifying and bottling the alchemy responsible for the performance of these two economies is proving difficult, and the so-called Beijing Consensus is a box waiting for usable content.

[14]See, for example, the positive assessment of recent performance and of promising trends by Radelet (2010).

Table 1.1 Average Annual GDP Growth, 1995–2001 and 2002–08

	Growth (%)	
Group	1995–2001	2002–08
GDP		
Low-income countries	4.7	5.9
Sub-Saharan Africa	3.5	5.2
World	3.0	3.1
Per capita GDP		
Low-income countries	2.3	3.7
Sub-Saharan Africa	0.8	2.7
World	1.6	1.8

Source: World Bank's World Development Indicators database.

Table 1.2 Average GDP Per Capita, 1995–2001 and 2002–08

	Amount (current US$)	
Group	1995–2001	2002–08
Low-income countries	286	405
Sub-Saharan Africa	530	846
World	5,181	7,088

Source: World Bank's World Development Indicators database.

Table 1.3 Average Share of Global GDP, 1995–2001 and 2002–08

	Share (%)	
Group	1995–2001	2002–08
Low-income countries	0.7	0.8
Sub-Saharan Africa	1.1	1.4

Source: World Bank's World Development Indicators database.

Moreover, a disproportionate share of the growth and employment[15] in Africa derives from nontradable government services and those provided by hotels and restaurants and by catering, security, construction, personal, janitorial, wholesale, and retail activities (table 1.4). Such services are a source of jobs but

---

[15]The informal sector is the source of a large number of jobs, most of which add little value but collectively account for a significant share of the "true" GDP.

Table 1.4 African Growth by Sector, 2002–07

Sector	Compound annual growth rate (%)
Hotels and restaurants	8.7
Transport and telecommunications	7.8
Construction	7.5
Utilities	7.3
Resources	7.1
Other services[a]	6.9
Wholesale and retail	6.8
Real estate and business services	5.9
Agriculture	5.5
Manufacturing	4.6
Public administration	3.9
Financial intermediation	2.4

Source: McKinsey Global Institute 2010.
Note: Data were calculated in 2005 U.S. dollars. The table covers 15 countries that together account for 80 percent of Africa's GDP: Algeria, Angola, Cameroon, the Arab Republic of Egypt, Ethiopia, Kenya, Libya, Morocco, Nigeria, Senegal, South Africa, Sudan, Tanzania, Tunisia, and Zimbabwe.
a. *Other services* include education, health, social services, and household services.

do not promise significant gain in either productivity or innovation.[16] Africa's growth potential from trade is also hampered by a product mix weighted with primary products, with the composition remaining more or less unchanged since 1995 (see tables A.1–A.5 in appendix A).

Other small economies in the middle-income range have also made limited headway in diversifying their top five exports. Between 1995 and 2009, Jordan, Mauritius, and Sri Lanka marked time, while countries such as Costa Rica, Morocco, and Tunisia did somewhat better, although their diversification was into higher-tech assembly activities that had low domestic value added (see tables A.6–A.11 in appendix A).

---

[16]Advanced countries such as the United States are in an uncomfortably similar situation, confronting sluggish job growth with the majority of jobs in nontradable services. According to Spence and Hlatshwayo (2011), 97 percent of the jobs created in the United States between 1990 and 2008 were in the nontradable sector, mainly in health care, government services, education, and retailing. Jensen (2011) provides a breakdown of increased employment in the United States in business services from 1997 through 2007, showing that the increase was fastest in real estate and leasing and slowest in finance, information, and management. He is more positive regarding the opportunities for growth and trade to be derived from business services.

Thus, a fresh look at the options for Sub-Saharan Africa—and other economies seeking to improve their growth prospects—in addition to the standard East Asian model is badly needed in light of the current understanding of growth dynamics and changing global circumstances.

Growth: The Stylized Facts

The literature on growth empirics is now so rich that a brief recapitulation of the stylized facts can suffice.[17]

For low- and middle-income countries, capital was the principal determinant of growth, with labor and total factor productivity (TFP) trailing well behind. Since 1989, capital investment can explain 45 percent of growth, with the bulk of this investment financed from domestic savings (see table 1.5, which provides data for the world as a whole, and figure 1.1, which gives a regional breakdown). Thus, domestic investment and savings are intertwined, with savings enabling investment but not causing it. Moreover, much of the investment in economies that grew most rapidly was financed through the own resources of firms and households or from bank borrowing—in the majority of cases from institutions owned or controlled by the state.[18]

Table 1.5   Contribution of Capital, Labor, and TFP to World Growth

	Share (%)		
	1989–95	**1995–2000**	**2000–06**
Capital	*54.1*	*46.4*	*40.7*
Information and communication technologies	12.8	15.6	11.7
Other	41.3	30.8	29.0
Labor	*29.6*	*30.4*	*23.6*
Hours	13.5	22.0	16.1
Quality	16.0	8.4	7.6
TFP	*16.3*	*23.2*	*35.7*

Source: Jorgenson and Vu 2009.

---

[17]Jones and Romer (2009, 3) provide a different set of stylized facts: (a) globalization and urbanization have enlarged the market; (b) growth has been accelerating over the centuries, and currently it tends to vary with respect to distances from the technology frontier; (c) factor inputs explain less than half the differences in per capita GDP; and (d) human capital per worker is rising, but the relative wages of skilled workers have not declined.

[18]Korea and Taiwan, China, began easing government control over the banking sector in the 1980s, but the influence of the state remained pervasive through the 1990s.

8

Figure 1.1 Sources of Economic Growth by Region, 1989–95 and 1995–2003

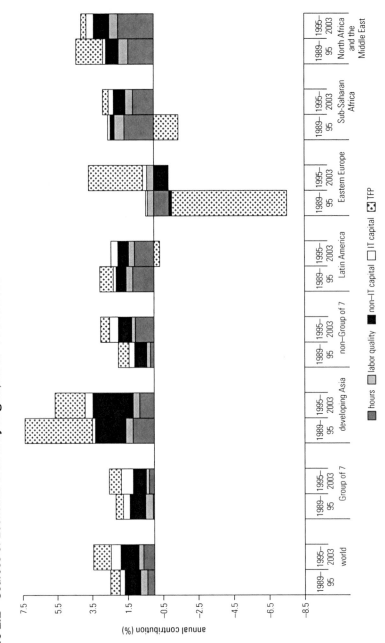

Source: Jorgenson 2006.

Between 1913 and 1950, the world economy grew by an average rate of 1.82 percent per year. During the second half of the 20th century, growth accelerated to 3.97 percent per year. This accelerated growth led to a sharp reduction in poverty despite much higher rates of population growth (Maddison 2003). The portion of the population in developing countries living on US$1 a day declined from 40 percent in 1981 to 18 percent in 2004 (Ferreira and Ravallion 2008). The reduction in absolute poverty was steepest in China and India, which registered the fastest economic growth rates. But some of the growth benefits have been undercut by rising inequality. Although global inequality changed little between 1980 and the early 2000s, inequality rose in 30 of the 49 countries for which data are available covering the 1990 to 2004 period (Ferreira and Ravallion 2008; Firebaugh and Goesling 2007). Interestingly, thus far, changes in equality seem not to be systematically related to growth or to civic unrest and civil wars (de Dominicis, de Groot, and Florax 2006; Ferreira and Ravallion 2008; Voitchovsky 2011).

Upper-middle-income and high-income countries are deriving more of their growth from gains in TFP, and the consensus view among researchers is that, over the longer run, growth is a function of TFP (see figure 1.1).[19] It is helpful to keep this in perspective. Jorgenson, Ho, and Samuels (forthcoming) estimate that increasing TFP contributed just 12 percent to U.S. growth between 1960 and 2007, capital contributed 60 percent, and the balance was attributable to labor. However, they acknowledge that growth over the longer term will hinge on productivity enhancing innovation in a few sectors, among which computer production and use and agriculture could be prominent: "Although innovation accounts for a relatively minor portion of economic growth [over the past five decades], this portion is vital for maintaining gains in the U.S. standard of living in the long run" (Jorgenson, Ho, and Samuels, forthcoming).

Total factor productivity (or multifactor productivity) has long been a catchall for gains from innovation in a variety of areas, the measurement and individual

---

[19]Comin and Hobijin (2010) observe that differences in the levels of per capita GDP are mostly explained by varying levels of TFP. They then go on to show that rates of growth are also substantially related to the rates of TFP increase, which, in turn, depend on the speed with which countries adopt technologies and narrow gaps. According to findings reported by Hulten (2009), TFP explained one-half of the growth in the United States between 1995 and 2005, but only one-fifth of the growth in the EU—which in the aggregate was one-half of the growth achieved by the United States. Growth in the EU relied more on capital and on non–information and communication technology capital. However, once the contribution of intangibles to growth is factored in, the share of TFP in the United States drops to 35 percent, and the role of information and communication technology capital is also diminished. The contribution of TFP to growth once intangibles are included is low in both Japan and the United Kingdom.

contributions of which have proven difficult to pin down.[20] However, these gains are the key policy targets, and the most interesting research on the sources of growth is precisely on these elusive "quarks."[21] There are many quarks, but six are most amenable to policy action: (a) human capital, variously measured,[22] and its quality; (b) technological capability and entrepreneurship and their enhancement through information technology (IT);[23] (c) networking; (d) managerial skills and other intangibles determining organizational effectiveness; (e) institutions affecting incentives, competition, allocative efficiency, and governance; and (f) the characteristics of urbanization.[24] Typically, all six affect production and use of knowledge, resource allocation, and productive utilization. The final section of the chapter discusses these factors further.

Growth has been spearheaded in the earlier stages of development by the industrial sector in almost all countries (UNIDO 2009), and though services are the leading source of growth and employment as economies mature,[25] industry

---

[20]Although TFP occupies center stage, its slipperiness remains an issue. Growth theorists have struggled to arrive at precise estimates and to isolate the contribution of research and development and of innovation. TFP is not only about technological change, but precise decomposition runs into a thicket of conceptual and statistical problems. A quote from Jorgenson, Ho, and Samuels (forthcoming) can help thread productivity, innovation, and quarks together. They state, "Productivity growth is the key indicator of innovation. Economic growth can take place without innovation through replication of established technologies. Investment increases the availability of these technologies, while the labor force expands as population grows. With only replication and without innovation, output will increase in proportion to capital and labor inputs. By contrast, the successful introduction of new products and new or altered processes, organization structures, systems, and business models generates growth of output that exceeds the growth of capital and labor inputs."

[21]The analogy with the quarks being chased by physicists for decades is arguably not farfetched. Measuring the contribution of quarks is a source of immense econometric frustration. Ciccone and Jarocinski (2009) determined that every change in growth data or change in the sample causes apparently robust results to disappear and new quarks to replace old quarks. Thus, from among the almost 150 variables tested in growth regressions, the "real quarks" are still giving researchers a run for their money.

[22]Measurement of human capital remains contested territory. As Aghion and others (2009, 1) note, "the relationship between education and growth . . . is fragile at best" because tests run afoul of reverse causality, the use of crude proxies for human capital, and the neglect of intermediating variables that determine how education affects growth.

[23]For more about this quark, see Brynjolfsson and Saunders (2010). Between 1995 and 2007, IT-producing and IT-using industries were the principal sources of U.S. growth.

[24]By conceptualizing and estimating the magnitude of intangibles, Corrado, Hulten, and Sichel (2009) show that they raised U.S. growth by 10 percent during 1995 to 2003.

[25]However, in several late-starting economies with small industrial sectors, services—because of their share in the economy—are responsible for much of the growth.

remains the more productive and innovative of the two major sectors.[26] Meanwhile, the share of agriculture in GDP everywhere shrinks to relative insignificance, although in Asia and Africa, most of the population is nonurban and its livelihood depends on agriculture and affiliated activities. The recent experience of India, Ireland, and some of the smaller countries in Eastern Europe points to the growth potential inherent in tradable impersonal services and of software.[27] For small economies, service-led growth, backstopped by investment in computer literacy, IT, and associated skills, is a real possibility, and for large economies, such growth is a necessary complement to the impetus from other sectors.[28]

Some countries, including many in Africa and the Middle East, have derived much of their growth from the development and export of natural resource–based products, whether minerals or agricultural commodities. In most instances, mineral (including energy) extraction and its beneficiation, if any, has been paced by foreign investment and has created enclave sectors that are loosely linked to the rest of the economy and generate few spillovers. Although natural resources can boost economic performance and supplement other sources of growth (as has been the case, for instance, in Malaysia and Indonesia), absent a sound, forward-looking policy environment, large mineral resources can inhibit industrialization and growth by encouraging nontradable activities and by appreciating the real exchange rate. This phenomenon, which is variously described as the "resource curse"[29] or "Dutch disease," has attracted an immense volume of research, but Lederman and Maloney (2008) have questioned whether the longer-term consequences of resource booms for growth are necessarily negative.

Although the bulk of aggregate demand derives from consumption followed by investment, many economies, small and large, have supplemented these sources with demand arising from trade. The smaller open and rapidly growing economies have relied (usually for brief periods) on net exports for as much as 40 percent of their overall GDP growth, with 20 percent being closer to the norm (see figure 1.2). Imports have played an almost equally important role, because they are vehicles for

---

[26]Innovation in services is harder to nail down and frequently is not patented. But it may be speeding up and, in the process, displacing thousands of workers doing routine work that newly developed algorithms and machine intelligence can readily undertake. See Brynjolfsson and McAfee (2011) and Arthur (2011) on the "Second Economy."

[27]See Ghani (2010) on how services are revolutionizing India's trade prospects. The prospects of growing services exports (particularly those of the United States) are examined in detail by Jensen (2011).

[28]See McKinsey Global Institute (2010) on the contribution of services to growth and employment in developed and middle-income economies.

[29]Researchers refer to a mineral resource and energy resource curse and a political resource curse. See Humphreys, Sachs, and Stiglitz (2007) on how countries have avoided the resource curse or minimized its impact. See also Frankel (2010) for a review of resource-based development.

Figure 1.2 Percentage Point Contribution of Real Net Exports to GDP Growth in Asia, 1995–2000 and 2000–06

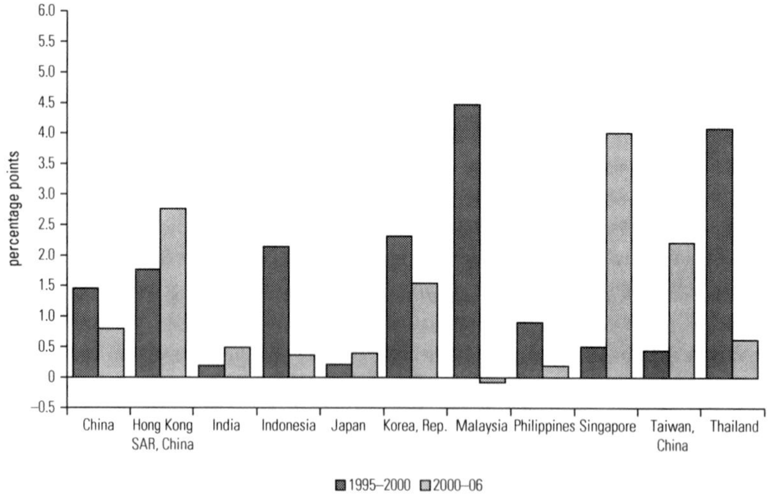

Source: Haltmaier and others 2007, 54.
Note: China and India data are only through 2005.

technology transfer and contribute to technological catch-up (Ding and Knight 2008; Lawrence and Weinstein 2001). Thus, tradable goods and services—mainly manufactures and resource-based products—have underpinned the rapid growth of economies that were able to create a production base of sufficient size through domestic investment, financed in large part from national savings.

Foreign direct investment (FDI) in production facilities, infrastructure, and research and development has supplemented domestic investment as well as technology transfer through trade and indigenous efforts at building innovation capacity. The contribution of FDI has rarely exceeded 5 percent of GDP, although in a number of the most successful economies, foreign investment was significantly higher,[30] and it catalyzed industrialization, helped to promote exports, contributed to an upgrading of the product mix, and is leading to a global distribution of the value chain (see Smeets 2008).

For the past three decades, growth has been powerfully aided by the integration of the global economy. In particular, trade liberalization[31] and measures that have eased

---

[30]Vietnam is one such example. See Nguyen (2006).

[31]Tariffs on manufactured goods fell from an average of 40 percent when the General Agreement on Tariffs and Trade was signed in 1947 to 5 percent in 2000. A compelling definition of *globalization* by Flynn and Giráldez (2004, 83) is the establishment of permanent trade relations among all segments of the world economy, thereby leading to "an exchange of products continuously and on a scale that generates deep and lasting impacts on all trading partners."

the flow of capital,[32] the circulation of skills,[33] and the sharing of information have stimulated economic performance directly and through a variety of externalities.

Last but not least, the golden age of growth (since 1950) is indebted to the incentives, innovations, and productivity gains arising from a number of general-purpose technologies (GPTs).[34] Two GPTs that have been at the forefront are the semiconductors and IT and of computers and the Internet. These GPTs are the signature technologies of recent times, and each has spawned a host of productivity-enhancing innovations affecting a wide range of activities (Jovanovic and Rousseau 2005).[35] As Martin Kenney (1997, 95) observes, "Electronics is being driven not by discrete innovations but rather by incessant waves of branching innovations that are generating a constantly proliferating range of products. Through this process new industry sectors are being created, separated, and merged. The increased processing power and functionality of new products in turn permit new tasks to be undertaken by machines. These new capabilities rapidly become needs. For example, whereas an Internet link was formerly a luxury for engineers, scientists, and a few computer buffs, it is rapidly becoming a necessity."[36]

---

[32]Mishkin (2005) maintains that financial globalization positively influences development but can also trigger crises such as the one that pummeled the global economy from 2008 to 2009. Following that crisis, many researchers view the contribution of financial innovations and of financial integration in a different light, given the inadequacy of regulatory mechanisms in most countries and the immense political clout wielded by large financial entities. See Lerner and Tufano (2011).

[33]Skill circulation occurs through brain drain, brain gain, and brain circulation.

[34]A survey of the literature on GPTs and of past GPTs can be found in Lipsey, Carlaw, and Bekar (2005). Most GPTs play the role of "enabling technologies opening up new opportunities rather than offering complete final solutions. For example, electric motors fostered the more efficient design of factories [and] users of microelectronics benefit from the surging power of silicon by wrapping around integrated circuits, their own technical advances" (Bresnahan and Trajtenberg 1995, 84). The infiltration of small, low-cost microprocessors, such as Intel's Atom, into treadmills, billboards, coffee machines, and gas dispensers shows how the evolution and diffusion of this protean technology is continuing, driven by cost and other innovations (King 2010).

[35]The productivity of these GPTs (as was the case earlier with electrical technology) is magnified, and the number of crossover innovations is enhanced, by the increase in knowledge capital and by an open and competitive environment that is furnished with intellectual property institutions and is conducive to innovation (Lo and Sutthiphisal 2010).

[36]In fields such as genetics, biology, climatology, and the social sciences, research is being rendered more productive through innovative uses of computing power to automate the framing and testing of multiple hypotheses with the help of advances in data processing; evaluative algorithms (earlier artificial intelligence programs included Prospector, Bacon, and Fahrenheit); and robotic systems. The latest programs for biological experiments "step through activities needed to conduct a continuously looping procedure that starts with question, carries out experiments to answer the question, evaluates the results, and reformulates new questions" (Waltz and Buchanan 2009, 43; see also Glymour 2004).

Hunting for Quarks

The factors described in the previous section constitute the determinants of growth from the side of supply and the side of demand. From the perspective of longer-term growth and its sustainability, capital, labor, and the factors influencing TFP are more relevant for policy-making purposes. Here the discourse on growth becomes intertwined with that of development, and one can see the growth pathway becoming one with the development pathway.

Inside the TFP Black Box

Increasing capital investment in productive activities and maximizing the return from this investment must necessarily be the focus of growth-enhancing policies. The evidence from theory and from East Asian experience suggests that accelerating growth and maintaining a higher tempo depends on an upward shift in the rate of capital accumulation. All of the fast-growing Asian economies relied on higher rates of investment than the average rate for developing countries. Japan led the way, followed by Korea and the first cohort of "tiger economies." Approximately a decade and a half later, the second cohort of Southeast Asian tigers imitated the first. Investment propensities were buttressed by governments that were committed to economic development and were able to back up words with policies that resulted in macroeconomic and political stability and that reduced business risks.[37] Development of the banking sector and improved access to term and trade financing through public and private channels, a widening of the domestic market (and a larger middle class), and expanding opportunities to sell overseas attracted investors, while the strengthening of market institutions reduced entry barriers and stimulated competition.[38]

By current standards and criteria, the investment climate in the tiger economies was a great deal worse than is the average climate in developing countries today, but this problem did not prevent investment from surging forward.[39] Similarly, the business climate was distinctly unpropitious in India when investment began rising after 2000 and in Vietnam following the initiation of (Doi Moi)

---

[37]As Acemoğlu (2009, 1) bluntly put it, "Nations are not like children—they are not born rich or poor. Their governments make them that way."

[38]OECD (2006) provides a detailed survey of entry barriers, including a discussion of both structural barriers (resulting from industry conditions linked to scale economies and network effects, for example) and strategic barriers (created by the actions of market participants through exclusive dealings, for example).

[39]East Asian developmental states were able to mobilize savings for investment purposes using publicly owned banks (as in China, Korea, and Taiwan, China); public pension funds requiring mandatory contributions (as in Malaysia and Singapore); postal savings systems (as in Japan); and state-controlled insurance schemes and budget-financed national investment funds (as in Korea).

reforms in 1986. The initial policy lesson to be drawn from East Asian experience is that governments committed to development, able to provide leadership, and equipped with the instruments to ensure stability can, with some help from FDI and trading opportunities, initiate long-lasting virtuous growth spirals. In fact, Asian successes in the 1970s through the first half of the 1990s had little to do with the sophistication of policy tools, with logistics and supply-chain management, or with technological innovation.[40] Apart from macropolicies to contain inflation, governments relied on tax exemptions, directed credit, and exchange rate incentives to encourage investors. They then deployed other longer-range measures to sustain performance. The really interesting lessons from the history of rapidly growing economies are not so much about macropolicies or the factors responsible for the state of the business climate; rather, they are about the measures that triggered a rapid improvement in the business climate and motivated investment behavior over an extended period of time, that contributed to technological catch-up and some incremental process innovation,[41] that spurred incremental innovation in a number of interlinked areas, and that enabled structural changes—including, most notably, a rapid and orderly transfer of labor from the primary sector to expanding urban centers. Together these measures reinforced the growth from capital investment by helping to raise factor productivity.

Successful developers have emphasized to varying degrees five objectives (the elusive quarks) in their pursuit of growth, all of which relate back to the drivers of TFP identified previously:

- Forging a consensus around an outward-oriented growth strategy
- Crafting the institutional infrastructure for a competitive economy in coordination with labor, the business community, and other stakeholders while strengthening the administrative capabilities of the state to frame and implement policies[42]
- Creating an open, networked "learning economy"[43] so as to build human capital of the requisite quality, make it easier to absorb ideas and technologies, increase the horizontal diversity of research lines and the establishment of new lines of inquiry, enhance production capabilities through a freer circulation of tacit knowledge, and increase the fruitfulness of domestic innovation (Murray and others 2009)

---

[40]However, declining transportation costs stimulated trade worldwide.

[41]According to Parente and Prescott (2000), impediments to technology adoptions are among the principal causes of lagging performance.

[42]Jagdish Bhagwati (2010) associates policy making with three *i*'s: ideas, institutions, and interests or interest groups.

[43]Several different facets of the learning economy viewed in the context of globalization are discussed in Archibugi and Lundvall (2001).

- Stimulating entrepreneurship[44] and organizational efficiency
- Internalizing entrepreneurship and organizational efficiency within an expanding urban system that is conducive to spillovers and maximizes agglomeration economies

Long-Term Strategy and Coordination

A modern market economy is an exceedingly complex organism, and for it to deliver above-normal growth and productivity outcomes over a period spanning decades, the state and other significant stakeholders must envision longer-term strategies and attempt to mesh these strategies so that the state can arrive at and effectively implement sound policies. When investment—whether physical or human—and technology are the central elements of strategies, the government needs to be active in coordinating the workings of at least four other bodies: (a) key segments of the business community suitably represented by chambers of industry, business associations, and developers with substantial voice and authority; (b) labor unions or other influential representatives able to communicate the concerns of workers and exercise a degree of discipline over their constituency; (c) the financial community in countries where banks and other major financial entities are privately owned or controlled by foreign shareholders; and (d) the education sector (or, more broadly, the learning economy, which includes preschooling and vocational training), because that sector is responsible for the skills that industry needs if it is to produce, absorb technologies, and conduct research and is a source of ideas to underpin technological advances.

Several of the smaller economies—Finland, Ireland, and Singapore among them—have devised consultative arrangements with these other entities to facilitate coordination, to enable the government to achieve a workable consensus on economic objectives and strategies, and to agree on emergency remedial policies when the nation faces crisis. Almost every country has devised various consultative arrangements with major stakeholders, but few of these arrangements deliver results. In many cases, governments lack the capability to strategize and implement policies. Framing strategies and coordinating plans might also not be a priority for the business sector; sometimes relations can turn adversarial and hostile, and communication breaks down. Not infrequently, elected officials and government agencies are captured by powerful, rent-seeking elements from the business and financial communities.[45] Effective coordination in the interests of long-term growth is something of an art. Peter Evans (1995) believes that it is a function of the "embeddedness" of key government agencies in the business environment,

---

[44]Schoar (2009) differentiates between transformational and subsistence entrepreneurship, with the former being the kind countries want to increase.

[45]Regulatory capture is almost the rule rather than the exception in developed economies as well as developing ones.

combined with autonomy to formulate strategy, provide leadership, and build alliances. There are other formulas as well, but needless to say, the coordination of activities and the conduct of policy so as to realize developmental objectives are critical to achieving an above-average economic performance.[46] Governments that lack the political will, the organizational capability, and the expertise to coordinate and implement risk being caught in what Pritchett, Woolcock, and Andrews (2010) label "state capability traps."

Learning Economy

The learning economy has several parts, starting with the schooling (including preschooling[47]) system and including the vocational training, tertiary education, and research conducted in universities and public institutes, as well as by domestic and foreign businesses; lifelong learning; and the harnessing of digital intelligence and artificial intelligence with the help of a state-of-the-art IT network. Supplementing these facets is the scientific acculturation imparted by science centers, museums, science exhibitions, and public lectures. Countries initially focus on primary and secondary schooling before devoting attention to the vocational and higher tiers of the education system. What differentiates high-achieving countries from others is the subsequent stress on the quality of schooling at all levels; the resources devoted to increasing access to tertiary education, to developing research universities, and to enhancing research capacity in the economy at large; and the importance such countries attach to bolstering learning and innovation by investing lavishly in IT capacity and encouraging its deep assimilation.[48] Many countries (China being an outstanding example) are hard at work fashioning a learning economy[49] and inducing links between entities conducting research and training on the one hand and firms on the other. From among them, the front-runners in Europe are Finland and Ireland, whereas in East Asia, Korea and Singapore have pulled ahead of the rest. Each of these countries is anchoring sustainable growth to its own version of a learning economy.[50]

---

[46]Rodrik (2005) has repeatedly emphasized this point.

[47]A child's initial skill set is correlated with family attributes such as the education of parents and maternal nurturing. These attributes are largely beyond the reach of policy (Cunha and others 2006).

[48]By training more engineers, Finland increased patenting activity, according to research by Toivanen and Väänänen (2011).

[49]The outstanding and top-ranked scores of 15-year-olds from Shanghai on the 2009 Programme for International Student Assessment tests demonstrate how much can be achieved in a short span of time through determined effort.

[50]A study of crossover innovations following the introduction and spread of electricity points to the importance of human capital and of the learning environment in stimulating invention (Lo and Sutthiphisal 2010).

Entrepreneurship and Management

Investment activity and the translation of ideas into commercially successful technologies is the work of entrepreneurs and managers. Entrepreneurs, whether in the private sector or in the public sector, have a key role in determining how much capital accumulation takes place and its sectorwide distribution. Both of these factors affect growth. Entrepreneurs also bring ideas and technologies into the marketplace and test their commercial worth. If entrepreneurship is weak, technological change and innovation also slow, irrespective of the stock of technologies waiting to be exploited and also of the productivity of domestic research activities.[51] Dynamic economies are necessarily highly entrepreneurial ones with a culture that strongly rewards initiative and risk taking and is relatively tolerant of failure.[52] The challenges for late-starting economies are how to inculcate a more vibrant entrepreneurial culture in the private and public domains[53] through wider participation, especially of the highly educated elites and members of the diaspora, and how to partially erase the stigma associated with the failure of businesses. Failure is a powerfully inhibiting factor in many countries, because four out of five start-up activities do fail within a couple of years. Thus, giving the unbowed entrepreneurs additional chances (including access to credit) is vital if business activity is to flourish in good times and revive quickly after bad times.

Entrepreneurship needs to be complemented by deep managerial skills if it is to sustain business performance beyond the start-up phase and grow companies, to fully exploit the potential of mainstream as well as frontier technologies, and to wring the maximum productivity from factor inputs.[54] Research has consistently underscored the wide differences in productivity and profitability among firms within the same industry in a single country, where all have access to a common technology set. The bulk of these differences are ascribed to the quality of management, which is determined by training, experience, and the incentive environment within a firm, the industry, and the market at large. Clearly training matters, but the other two factors are no less significant. The desirable mix will differ among countries, and achieving it is a complex endeavor that depends partly on policy and institutions and partly also on the competitive forces at work in the business community.

---

[51]Japan now confronts this problem as it struggles to break away from two decades of slow growth.

[52]Tolerance of failure does not imply that ineptitude is not penalized.

[53]The scale and diverse activities of the public sector in most countries makes it essential to infuse dynamism into public bodies.

[54]Entrepreneurs who start up firms rarely prove to be good managers who can help firms to grow.

Competition and Openness

The next issue is market conditions influencing openness and competition. Although the advantages of competition have long been recognized, and openness—especially to trade—is accepted as a means of stimulating competition, technology transfer, technological spillovers, productivity gains, and faster growth, policy makers must struggle against vested interests and newly emerging demands for protection if they are to dismantle existing barriers to trade and curb the emergence of new barriers. It is the same with domestic competition. Theory is relatively explicit in its support for untrammeled competition, but practice is fraught with complications. Certain natural monopolies need to be regulated, and regulation of many other industries (to protect consumers) has a bearing on the degree of competition. Laws governing competition and their interpretation and implementation by the courts also determine the decisions and behavior of firms. It appears that small economies that are highly dependent on trade are more likely to favor competitive policies and institutions, often because they have little choice. But even in small economies, public ownership; procurement practices; local regulations and standards; labor market rules affecting the entry, growth, and exit of firms; and financial market constraints can selectively dampen competition, the turnover of firms, and the emergence of "global champions." The test for policy makers seeking to maximize productivity and technological gains is to strive after the goal of a competitive market economy but to be mindful of the need to accommodate industrial adjustment as well as the orderly exit of firms, both large and small; the transitory concerns of infant industries; the desirability of nurturing new technologies; and the avoidance of finance- and regulation-induced asset bubbles, which are a prelude to crises.

The Networked Economy

The literature on development is giving greater attention to networking,[55] with the focus increasingly on the urban sector, where agglomeration stimulates productive and innovative activities through local and global networking. With urban populations growing, urban GDP accounting for between 60 and 80 percent of GDP, and the Internet having created a host of globe-spanning communities, networking is a force to be reckoned with.[56] Cities are as old as civilization, but as densely networked drivers of growth, cities have arrived fairly recently on the

---

[55]Castells and Himanen (2002) discuss the Finnish model of a networked, information-based welfare state and compare it with Singapore and Silicon Valley to show how they emerged from different starting points.

[56]Manuel Castells (2000) was among the earliest to draw attention to the emergence of the globe-spanning, information-driven network society.

policy landscape. It was long apparent that industry concentrated in urban centers and that there was a correlation between urbanization and development;[57] however, during the past 20 years, research has accumulated showing that industrial composition and the size of cities can raise productivity through agglomeration, urbanization, and scale economies reinforced by knowledge diffusion through networking.[58] The productivity of cities is thus a complex outcome of several factors, with livability, cultural and recreational amenities, and openness seen as contributing to learning, local innovation, and start-up activities.[59]

These findings require that policies related to growth, productivity, and innovation factor in the contributory role of the urban environment. Growth, learning, and innovation strategies must now be jointly cast within an urban framework, and the success of policies to raise growth and to promote technological change is interlinked with the characteristics, quality, and

---

[57]Polèse (2005, 1430) noted that many studies have "repeatedly demonstrated the disproportionate contribution of urban areas to national income and product." For example, "greater São Paulo accounted for 8.6 percent of Brazil's population but generated 36.1 percent of national GDP. For all nations, the contribution of urban areas to GDP or income is greater than their share of the national population." UN (2008) describes how the wealth of nations is concentrated in metropolitan cities, with cities such as Seoul, Bangkok, São Paulo, and Karachi accounting for a disproportionate share. See also Henderson (2010).

[58]The largest cities are the most influential in creating spillovers in information and technology. These knowledge spillovers in larger urban areas also increase the rate of firm creation in emerging industries (Polèse 2005). Carlino, Chatterjee, and Hunt (2007) find that patenting rises with increasing employment intensity in cities. And Cortright and Mayer (2001) observe not only that patenting and venture funding are concentrated in a few metropolitan areas in the United States but also that most patents are issued to a handful of firms. This finding is confirmed by Acs, Anselin, and Varga (2001), who observe a clustering of patents in 10 states and in a few counties within those states. Not surprisingly, the leading metro areas in the United States are also the principal sources of the nation's manufactured exports, accounting for 62 percent of total exports (Istrate, Rothwell, and Katz 2010). A networking of things via information and communication technology could take productivity to an even higher plane, for example, through smart roadways and electronic communications among vehicles and between vehicles and sources of information that would affect the decisions of drivers.

[59]Ten large metro regions in the United States are responsible for a third of all patents, and the research on agglomeration economies has pointed to the productivity gains that can accrue to large cities from scale, diversity, and density of activities and from the apparent superlinearity (albeit modest) of innovations in relation to the size of the city (Carlino, Chatterjee, and Hunt 2007; Carlino and Hunt 2009).

ease of networking.[60] If cities do not actively enable economic change, growth will falter. This observation represents a new departure in thinking that is slowly being internalized: the pathway to growth runs through industrial and networked cities.

Looking at the "Sifire" Family of Models

The five drivers of TFP—and of growth more broadly—direct our attention to the experience of countries widely considered as being in a class of their own by having compressed development into a remarkably short period of time, mainly by massively upgrading human resources and harnessing knowledge capital to the fullest extent.[61] Capital was no less important for these countries, but the speed of technological catch-up, which was made possible by investment in the learning economy and in institutional and organizational capabilities and technology, significantly increased the return from capital. The three economies that are the dramatis personae of this study are Singapore, Finland, and Ireland, referred to collectively as the *Sifire group*, or *Sifire* for short.

Why select these countries and not others? There are several reasons. Between 1985 and 2005, the three Sifire countries demonstrated a remarkable capacity to learn and, by improving the quality of learning, to achieve technological catch-up, develop manufacturing capabilities of the first rank, and increase their ability to innovate. Demographically, they are of comparable size. Ireland, the smallest, had a population of 4.4 million in 2008, as compared with 5.3 million for Finland, the largest of the three countries (table 1.6).[62] In 1985, Sifire could be classified as middle income, with per capita GDPs ranging from US\$6,000 to US\$11,000. By

---

[60]The "creative classes" will gather in selected urban centers, and the historical function of cities is to act as gathering places for the best and the brightest (Florida 2002). Hidalgo (2010a) describes how a network contributes to the diffusion of development through the product space. He notes that the value is in the network connecting different parts rather than in the individual factors and components. "Firms and institutions are not only large collections of individuals. They are networks of individuals that interact through hierarchies, but mostly despite them. The ability of a firm to be productive depends not only on the talents of its employees, but largely on the way they interact" (Hidalgo 2010b, 2). In the same way, the effectiveness of urban networks can be a determinant of the productivity and innovativeness of the city.

[61]See Ashton and others (2002) on how the East Asian tiger economies managed this achievement.

[62]Small countries have proliferated since the middle of the 20th century, and of the 193 independent countries that exist today, 87 have populations of less than 5 million. Hence, the Sifire group is representative of a large number of economies, extending from the very poor to the richest (that is, Luxembourg, which had a population of just 400,000 in 2009 and a per capita GDP of US\$80,000).

Table 1.6   Population of the Sifire Group, 1985 and 2008

	Population	
Country	1985	2008
Finland	4,902,000	5,313,399
Ireland	3,540,000	4,425,675
Singapore	2,736,000	4,839,400

Source: World Bank's World Development Indicators database.

2008, they were among the countries with the highest incomes as a result of steady and relatively high rates of growth in per capita incomes (table 1.7).[63] Singapore's economy grew the fastest on average, followed by Ireland's, with Finland's economy in third place (table 1.8).[64] The growth performance of Sifire was closely linked to competitiveness, derived in large part from institutional factors and the quality of the countries' human resources. Of the three countries, Singapore has been in the lead since 1989 according to all criteria, followed by Finland and Ireland. Table 1.9 provides rankings for 1989 and 1992, and table 1.10 presents the rankings for 2003. Aside from competitiveness in general, the countries had high scores for government and business efficiency, both of which have underpinned economic performance.

Sifire countries share structural characteristics, and their economic performance, which is significantly buoyed by the opportunities presented by regional and global markets, places them in the ranks of the world's most successful economies. These similarities are convenient for the purposes of analysis and the teasing out of lessons for potential fast followers.[65] The political and economic diversity of the Sifire group adds richness to the lessons. Singapore, a city-state,

---

[63]Here is how Ireland's leading historian Robert Fitzroy Foster (2008, 7) describes the decade extending from 1995 to 2005: "Output . . . increased by 350 percent, . . . personal disposable income doubled, exports increased fivefold, trade surpluses accumulated into billions, employment boomed, immigrants poured into the country. . . . The country had apparently become vastly rich."

[64]A decomposition of growth rates by Crafts (2008) indicates that between 1990 and 2003 TFP rose fastest in Ireland (2.24 percent per year); Finland was next, with TFP growing 1.49 percent; and Singapore, whose TFP increased by 0.9 percent, followed. Ireland's economy more than tripled in nominal terms between 1990 and 2003, and exports grew by 4.5 times. (Harris 2005).

[65]*Fast followers* is a term used to describe firms in Taiwan, China, which have shown themselves unusually quick to absorb and advance technologies. See Kraemer and others (1996) and Mathews (2005).

Table 1.7   GDP Per Capita of the Sifire Group, 1985 and 2008

Country	Amount (US$)	
	1985	2008
Finland	11,253	51,323
Ireland	5,826	60,460
Singapore	6,485	37,597

Source: World Bank's World Development Indicators database.

Table 1.8   Average Annual GDP Growth of the Sifire Group, 1985–2008

Country	Growth (%)			
	1985–89	1995–99	2000–04	2005–08
Finland	4.0	4.6	2.9	3.2
Ireland	3.7	9.5	6.2	4.3
Singapore	6.4	6.0	5.0	5.9

Source: World Bank's World Development Indicators database.

Table 1.9   IMD World Competitiveness Rankings of the Sifire Group, 1989 and 1992

Country	Dynamism of the economy	Human resources	Overall ranking
1989			
Finland	5	7	6
Ireland	10	17	16
Singapore	1	1	1
1992			
Finland	11	9	10
Ireland	4	10	9
Singapore	1	1	1

Source: IMD 2010.
Note: In 1989, country rankings were calculated for two separate groups: (a) 23 member countries of the Organisation for Economic Co-operation and Development (including Finland and Ireland) and (b) 10 newly industrialized countries (including Singapore). In 1992, the same division of groups applied, except that Pakistan, South Africa, and the República Bolivariana de Venezuela were added to the second group.

uniquely highlights the extraordinary possibilities for well-managed and diversified industrial cities that creatively exploit the benefits of connectivity.

Finland demonstrates the workings of an advanced democratic system that has perfected the political and labor market institutions for consensus building around key economic objectives and the capacity to arrive at significant

Table 1.10   World Economic Forum and IMD Competitiveness Rankings of the Sifire Group, 2003

Country	World Economic Forum growth competitiveness index (2001–02)	IMD world competitiveness ranking (2003)	IMD business efficiency ranking (2003)	IMD government efficiency ranking (2003)
Finland	1	3	2	1
Ireland	11	11	6	13
Singapore	4	4	5	3

Sources: IMD 2010; WEF 2010.
Note: The World Economic Forum ranked 75 countries; IMD ranked 51 countries.

macroeconomic results by coordinating the initiatives of a number of small urban centers.

The success of Ireland, compared to that of the other two countries, was more a function of successful marketing and branding, access to the EU and its structural funds, and tax incentives for multinationals than of indigenous institutional innovation. The Ireland case brings out the mileage to be derived by a country that can turn itself into a regional hub by cleverly marketing location, low transaction costs, the quality of its workforce, and its urban assets. All three countries have also shown the extraordinary benefits derived from internal networking and networking with the international business and research communities. In the case of Ireland, in particular, such networking includes a well-placed diaspora of entrepreneurs and business people.

References

Acemoğlu, Daron. 2009. "What Makes a Nation Rich? One Economist's Big Answer." *Esquire*, November 18. http://www.esquire.com/features/best-and-brightest-2009/world-poverty-map-1209.

Acs, Zoltan J., Luc Anselin, and Attila Varga. 2001. "Patents and Innovation Counts as Measures of Regional Production of New Knowledge." Merrick School of Business, University of Baltimore. Baltimore MD.

Aghion, Philippe, Leah Boustan, Caroline Hoxby, and Jerome Vandenbussche. 2009. "The Causal Impact of Education on Economic Growth: Evidence from U.S." Brookings Papers on Economic Activity, Brookings Institution, Washington, DC.

Aghion, Philippe, and Steven Durlauf. 2009. "From Growth Theory to Policy Design." Commission on Growth and Development Working Paper 57, World Bank, Washington, DC.

Akamatsu, Kaname. 1962. "A Historical Pattern of Economic Growth in Developing Countries." *Developing Economies* 1 (1): 3–25.

Archibugi, Daniele, and Bengt-Åke Lundvall, eds. 2001. *The Globalizing Learning Economy.* Oxford, U.K.: Oxford University Press.

Arthur, Brian W. 2011. "The Second Economy." *McKinsey Quarterly* (October).

Ashton, David N., Francis Green, Johnny Sung, and Donna James. 2002. "The Evolution of Education and Training Strategies in Singapore, Taiwan, and South Korea: A Developmental Model of Skill Formation." *Journal of Education and Work* 15 (1): 5–30.

Bhagwati, Jagdish N. 2010. "Running in Place on Trade." *Project Syndicate*, July 20. http://www.project-syndicate.org.

Bresnahan, Timothy F., and Manuel Trajtenberg. 1995. "General Purpose Technologies: 'Engines of Growth'?" *Journal of Econometrics* 65 (1): 83–103.

Brynjolfsson, Erik, and Andrew McAfee. 2011. *Race against the Machine: How the Digital Revolution Is Accelerating Innovation, Driving Productivity, and Irreversibly Transforming Employment and the Economy*. Lexington, MA: Digital Frontier Press.

Brynjolfsson, Erik, and Adam Saunders. 2010. *Wired for Innovation: How Information Technology Is Reshaping the Economy*. Cambridge, MA: MIT Press.

Carlino, Gerald A., Satyajit Chatterjee, and Robert M. Hunt. 2007. "Urban Density and the Rate of Invention." *Journal of Urban Economics* 61 (3): 389–419.

Carlino, Gerald A., and Robert M. Hunt. 2009. "What Explains the Quantity and Quality of Local Inventive Activity?" Working Paper 09-12, Federal Reserve Bank of Philadelphia, Philadelphia, PA.

Castells, Manuel. 2000. *The Rise of the Network Society*. New York: Blackwell.

Castells, Manuel, and Pekka Himanen. 2002. *The Information Society and the Welfare State: The Finnish Model*. New York: Oxford University Press.

Ciccone, Antonio, and Marek Jarocinski. 2009. "Determinants of Economic Growth: Will Data Tell?" UPF Working Paper 1052, Universitat Pompeu Fabra, Barcelona, Spain.

Comin, Diego, and Bart Hobijin. 2010. "Technology Diffusion and Postwar Growth." NBER Working Paper 16378, National Bureau of Economic Research, Cambridge, MA.

Commission for Growth and Development. 2008. *The Growth Report: Strategies for Sustained Growth and Inclusive Development*. Washington, DC: World Bank.

Corrado, Carol, Charles R. Hulten, and Daniel Sichel. 2009. "Intangible Capital and U.S. Economic Growth." *Review of Income and Wealth* 55 (3): 661–85.

Cortright, Joseph, and Heike Mayer. 2001. "High Tech Specialization: A Comparison of High Technology Centers." Brookings Institution, Washington, DC.

Crafts, Nicholas. 2008. "The Celtic Tiger in Historical and International Perspective." Warwick Economic Research Paper 867, Department of Economics, University of Warwick, Coventry, U.K.

Cunha, Flavio, James J. Heckman, Lance Lochner, and Dimitriy V. Msterov. 2006. "Interpreting the Evidence on Life Cycle Skill Formation." In *Handbook of the Economics of Education*, ed. Eric A. Hanushek and Finis Welch, 697–812. Amsterdam: North-Holland.

de Dominicis, Laura, Henri de Groot, and Raymond Florax. 2006. "*Growth and Inequality: A Meta-Analysis.*" Discussion Paper 064/3, Tinbergen Institute, Amsterdam.

Ding, Sai, and John Knight. 2008. "*Why Has China Grown So Fast? The Role of Structural Change.*" Economic Series Working Paper 415, University of Oxford, Economics Department, Oxford, U.K.

Doucouliagos, Hristos, and Martin Paldam. 2009. "The Aid Effectiveness Literature: The Sad Results of 40 Years of Research." *Journal of Economic Surveys* 23 (3): 433–61.

Durlauf, Steven, Paul A. Johnson, and Jonathan R. W. Temple. 2004. *Growth Econometrics.* Madison: University of Wisconsin. http://www.ssc.wisc.edu/econ/archive/wp2004-18.pdf.

Easterly, William. 2009. "Economic Development Experts versus Economists: The Example of Industrial Policy." Presented at the World Bank, Washington, DC, September 14.

Evans, Peter. 1995. *Embedded Autonomy: States and Industrial Transformation.* Princeton, NJ: Princeton University Press.

Ferreira, Francisco H. G., and Martin Ravallion. 2008. "Global Poverty and Inequality: A Review of the Evidence." Policy Research Working Paper 4623, World Bank, Washington, DC.

Firebaugh, Glenn, and Brian Goesling. 2007. "Globalization and Global Inequalities: Recent Trends." In *The Blackwell Companion to Globalization,* ed. George Ritzer, 549–64. Malden, MA: Blackwell Publishing.

Florida, Richard. 2002. *The Rise of the Creative Class and How It's Transforming Work, Leisure, and Everyday Life.* New York: Basic Books.

Flynn, Dennis O., and Arturo Giráldez. 2004. "Path Dependence, Time Lags, and the Birth of Globalisation: A Critique of O'Rourke and Williamson." *European Review of Economic History* 8 (1): 81–108.

Foster, Robert Fitzroy. 2008. *Luck and the Irish: A Brief History of Change from 1970.* Oxford, U.K.: Oxford University Press.

Frankel, Jeffrey. 2010. *"The Natural Resource Curse: A Survey."* Faculty Research Working Paper 10-005, Harvard Kennedy School, Cambridge, MA.

Ghani, Ejaz. 2010. "The Service Revolution in India." VoxEU.org, September 25. http://www.voxeu.org/index.php?q=node/4673.

Ghemawat, Pankaj. 2011. *World 3.0: Global Prosperity and How to Achieve It.* Boston: Harvard Business School Press.

Glymour, Clark. 2004. "The Automation of Discovery." *Daedalus* 133 (1): 69–77.

Haltmaier, Jane T., Shaghil Ahmed, Brahima Coulibaly, Ross Knippenberg, Sylvain Leduc, Mario Marazzi, and Beth Anne Wilson. 2007. "The Role of China in Asia: Engine, Conduit, or Steamroller?" International Finance Discussion Paper 904, Board of Governors of the Federal Reserve System, Washington, DC.

Harris, William C. 2005. "Secrets of the Celtic Tiger: Act Two." *Issues in Science and Technology* (summer).

Hausmann, Ricardo, Lant Pritchett, and Dani Rodrik. 2005. "Growth Accelerations." *Journal of Economic Growth* 10 (4): 303–29.

Henderson, J. Vernon. 2010. "Cities and Development." *Journal of Regional Science* 50 (1): 515–40.

Hidalgo, César A. 2010a. "The Dynamics of Economic Complexity and the Product Space over a 42 Year Period." CID Working Paper 189, Center for International Development and Harvard Kennedy School, Harvard University, Cambridge, MA.

———. 2010b. "The Value in Links: Networks and the Evolution of Organizations." Center for International Development and Harvard Kennedy School, Harvard University, Cambridge, MA.

Hufbauer, Gary, and Kati Suominen. 2010. *Globalization at Risk: Challenges to Finance and Trade*. New Haven, CT: Yale University Press.

Hulten, Charles R. 2009. "Growth Accounting." NBER Working Paper 15341, National Bureau of Economic Research, Cambridge, MA.

Humphreys, Macartan, Jeffrey D. Sachs, and Joseph E. Stiglitz. 2007. *Escaping the Resource Curse*. New York: Columbia University Press.

IMD. 2010. *World Competitiveness Yearbook*. Lausanne, Switzerland: IMD.

Istrate, Emilia, Jonathan Rothwell, and Bruce Katz. 2010. "Export Nation: How U.S. Metros Lead National Export Growth and Boost Competitiveness." Metropolitan Policy Program, Brookings Institution, Washington, DC.

James, Harold. 2009. "The Late, Great Globalization." *Current History* 108 (714): 20–25.

Jensen, J. Bradford. 2011. *Global Trade in Services: Fear, Facts, and Offshoring*. Washington, DC: Peterson Institute of International Economics.

Jones, Charles I., and Paul M. Romer. 2009. "The New Kaldor Facts: Ideas, Institutions, Population, and Human Capital." NBER Working Paper 15094, National Bureau of Economic Resesarch, Cambridge, MA.

Jorgenson, Dale W. 2006. "Information Technology and the World Economy." Presented at the CEIR Lecture Series, Barcelona, Spain, May 11.

Jorgenson, Dale W., Mun S. Ho, and Jon Samuels. Forthcoming. "Information Technology and U.S. Productivity Growth." In *Industrial Productivity in Europe: Growth and Crisis*, ed. Matilde Mas and Robert Stehrer. Cheltenham, U.K.: Edward Elgar.

Jorgenson, Dale W., and Khuong M. Vu. 2009. "Growth Accounting within the International Comparison Program." *ICP Bulletin* 6 (1): 3–28.

Jovanovic, Boyan, and Peter L. Rousseau. 2005. "General Purpose Technologies." NBER Working Paper 11093, National Bureau of Economic Research, Cambridge, MA.

Kenney, Martin. 1997. "Value Creation in the Late Twentieth Century: The Rise of the Knowledge Worker." In *Cutting Edge: Technology, Information Capitalism, and Social Revolution*, ed. Jim Davis, Thomas Hirshl, and Michael Stack. New York: Verso Books.

King, Ian. 2010. "Intel Wants to Be Inside Everything." *Bloomberg Businessweek*, September 2. http://www.businessweek.com/magazine/content/10_37/b4194029898101.htm.

Kraemer, Kenneth L., Jason Dedrick, Chin-Yeong Hwang, Tze-Chen Tu, and Chee-Sing Yap. 1996. "Entrepreneurship, Flexibility, and Policy Coordination: Taiwan's Computer Industry." *Information Society* 12 (3): 215–49.

Landes, David. 1990. "Why Are We So Rich and They So Poor?" *American Economic Review* 80 (2): 1–13.

Lawrence, Robert Z., and David E. Weinstein. 2001. "Trade and Growth: Import-Led or Export Led?" In *Rethinking the East Asian Miracle*, ed. Joseph E. Stiglitz and Shahid Yusuf, New York: Oxford University Press.

Lederman, Daniel, and William Maloney. 2008. "In Search of the Missing Resource Curse." *Economía* 9 (1): 1–56.

Lerner, Josh, and Peter Tufano. 2011. "The Consequences of Financial Innovation: A Counterfactual Research Agenda." NBER Working Paper 16780, National Bureau of Economic Resesarch, Cambridge, MA.

Li, Wei, Taye Mengistae, and Lixin Colin Xu. 2011. "Diagnosing Development Bottlenecks: China and India." Policy Research Working Paper 56451, World Bank, Washington, DC.

Lipsey, Richard G., Kenneth I. Carlaw, and Clifford T. Bekar. 2005. *Economic Transformations: General Purpose Technologies and Long Term Economic Growth*. New York: Oxford University Press.

Lo, Shih-tse, and Dhanoos Sutthiphisal. 2010. "Crossover Inventions and Knowledge Diffusion of General Purpose Technologies: Evidence from the Electrical Technology." *Journal of Economic History* 70 (3): 744–64.

Maddison, Angus. 2003. *The World Economy: Historical Statistics*. Paris: OECD.

Mathews, John A. 2005. "The Intellectual Roots of Latecomer Industrial Development." *International Journal of Technology and Globalization* 1 (3–4): 433–50.

McKinsey Global Institute. 2010. "Lions on the Move: The Progress and Potential of African Economies." McKinsey & Company, Washington, DC.

Mishkin, Frederic. 2005. "Is Financial Globalization Beneficial." NBER Working Paper 11891, National Bureau of Economic Research, Cambridge, MA.

Murray, Fiona, Philippe Aghion, Mathias Dewatripont, Julian Kolev, and Scott Stern. 2009. "Of Mice and Academics: Examining the Effect of Openness on Innovation." NBER Working Paper 14819, National Bureau of Economic Resesarch, Cambridge, MA.

Nguyen, Lan Phi. 2006. "Foreign Direct Investment and Its Linkage to Economic Growth in Vietnam: A Provincial Level Analysis." Center for Regulation and Market Analysis, University of South Australia, Adelaide.

OECD (Organisation for Economic Co-operation and Development). 2006. *Barriers to Entry*. DAF/Comp(2005)42. Paris: OECD.

Parente, Stephen L., and Edward C. Prescott. 2000. *Barriers to Riches*. Cambridge, MA: MIT Press.

Polèse, Mario. 2005. "Cities and National Economic Growth: A Reappraisal." *Urban Studies* 42 (8): 1429–51.

Pritchett, Lant, Michael Woolcock, and Matt Andrews. 2010. "Capability Traps? The Mechanisms of Persistent Implementation Failure." Background paper for the *World Development Report 2011: Conflict, Security, and Development*, World Bank, Washington, DC.

Radelet, Stephen. 2010. *Emerging Africa: How 17 Countries Are Leading the Way*. Washington, DC: Center for Global Development.

Rodrik, Dani. 2005. "Growth Strategies." In *Handbook of Economic Growth*, ed. Philippe Aghion and Steven N. Durlauf, 967–1014. Amsterdam: North-Holland.

———. 2011. *The Globalization Paradox: Democracy and the Future of the World Economy*. New York: W.W. Norton.

Schoar, Antoinette. 2009. "The Divide between Subsistence and Transformational Entrepreneurship." Massachusetts Institute of Technology, Cambridge, MA.

Smeets, Roger. 2008. "Collecting the Pieces of the FDI Knowledge Spillovers Puzzle." *World Bank Research Observer* 23 (2): 107–38.

Solow, Robert M. 2007. "The Last 50 Years in Growth Theory and the Next 10." *Oxford Review of Economic Policy* 23 (1): 3–14.

Spence, Michael, and Sandile Hlatshwayo. 2011. "The Evolving Structure of the American Economy and the Employment Challenge." Working Paper, Council on Foreign Relations, New York.

Toivanen, Otto, and Lotta Väänänen. 2011. "Education and Invention." CEPR Discussion Paper 8537, Centre for Economic Policy Research, London.

UN (United Nations). 2008. *State of the World Cities 2010/2011: Cities for All: Bridging the Urban Divide.* Nairobi: United Nations.

UNIDO (United Nations Industrial Development Organization). 2009. *Industrial Development Report 2009: Breaking In and Moving Up—New Industrial Challenges for the Bottom Billion and the Middle-Income Countries.* Vienna: UNIDO.

Voitchovsky, Sarah. 2011. "Inequality, Growth, and Sectoral Change." In *The Oxford Handbook of Economics Inequality*, ed. Wiemer Salverda, Brian Nolan, and Timothy M. Smeeding. Oxford, U.K.: Oxford University Press.

Waltz, David, and Bruce G. Buchanan. 2009. "Automating Science." Science 324 (5923): 43–44.

WEF (World Economic Forum). 2010. *Global Competitiveness Report 2010–2011.* New York: World Economic Forum. http://www.weforum.org/reports.

Xu, Guo. 2011. "Growth Accelerations Revisited." Economic Journal Watch 8 (1): 39–56.

Yusuf, Shahid. 2009. *Development Economics through the Decades: A Critical Look at 30 Years of the World Development Report.* Washington, DC: World Bank.

2

How Sifire Compressed Development

To sustain high rates of growth, small economies must rely on exports because domestic markets are too quickly saturated. Exporting is easiest for resource-rich economies because there is a ready market for standardized commodities such as minerals and petroleum and because a sophisticated global marketing infrastructure is in place. Oil and gas producers such as Brunei Darussalam, Kuwait, Norway, and Qatar, as well as Botswana,[1] a producer of diamonds, have developed by exploiting their mineral wealth. An abundance of sparsely populated arable land is responsible for New Zealand's prosperity, which is based on the export of fruit, meat, and dairy products.[2] However, there are relatively few instances of small, resource-poor economies entering the ranks of high-income countries within two to three decades through the export of manufactures or services. Singapore, Finland, and Ireland (Sifire) are among the select group that beat the odds. Although each country's past is necessarily unique, there are enough overlapping strands and shared circumstances to construct a composite story highlighting the causal factors that affected all three economies to varying degrees—a story, moreover, that is of continuing relevance for low- and middle-income developing countries in the early decades of the 21st century.

---

[1]Botswana is one of two African countries belonging to the exclusive club of fast-growing economies, the other being Mauritius. See Beaulier (2003).

[2]New Zealand's largest firm is Fonterra, a dairy cooperative. Fonterra accounts for almost a third of global exports of dairy products.

Globalization: The Vital Backdrop

The 1980s are an appropriate starting point. That was when a second wave of globalization[3] was deriving momentum from trade liberalization, the loosening of capital controls, and the diffusion of innovations sparked by powerful new general-purpose technologies and, arguably, the Pax Americana.[4] The increase in cross-border trade, principally of manufactures and raw materials, stemmed from the confluence of several factors, among which four deserve special attention.

First, starting with the General Agreement on Tariffs and Trade (GATT), a series of international trade negotiations—with the Geneva Round in 1947 being the first[5]—were whittling away at the tariff and nontariff barriers to trade, and in the process, they widened the opportunities for export-oriented firms in the lower-middle-income and middle-income countries, which had begun building a competitive manufacturing base. Between 1980 and 1990, global trade rose by 5.0 percent per year. This figure accelerated to 6.1 percent from 1990 through 1995, and the completion of the Uruguay Round in 1993 further promoted liberalization.[6]

Second, a steady decline in the costs of surface transportation reinforced the effects of lower tariff barriers. This reduction in costs arose from technological advances such as containerization, ship design, and diesel engine technology and from advances in the handling of cargo at ports.[7] It was further aided by stable or

---

[3]An earlier wave crested at the beginning of the 20th century and was gradually reversed by the wars and depression that scarred the first five decades of that century.

[4]A number of the key global institutions such as the World Bank, the International Monetary Fund, the General Agreement on Tariffs and Trade, and the World Trade Organization were created by the United States through the exercise of its political power, and these institutions reflected the American vision of the world economy.

[5]Twenty-three countries met in Geneva to finalize the GATT in October 1947. Its initial benefits were enlarged through a series of eight trade rounds, culminating in Uruguay in 1993 with the creation of the World Trade Organization. The Doha Round, which started in 2001, is not yet concluded.

[6]According to Bordo and Rousseau (2011), trade liberalization was reinforced by the formation of the European Common Market and the gradual dismantling of capital controls after 1972.

[7]The modern shipping container (the workhorse 20-foot equivalent unit, or TEU) is the brainchild of Malcolm McLean, a trucker from North Carolina, who saw the container as a way of simplifying and speeding up the loading and unloading of cargo. Because of the TEU and associated innovations, the cost of shipping has fallen 10-fold since the late 1980s, and thanks to computers, shipping freight across the world has become a seamless, intricately choreographed activity, with loading, customs clearance, unloading, stacking, and placing containers on tractor trailers or railcars all precisely managed by computer systems (Levinson 2006). Huge container ships powered by mammoth diesels are the workhorses that haul the 20- and 40-foot containers across the oceans. And were it not for the advances in transport technologies and computerization, East Asia would have struggled to become the workshop of the world, and international trade would have never scaled these dizzying heights (Smil 2010).

declining prices for fossil fuels. The costs of air shipment declined 2.52 percent annually from 1980 to 1993 with the entry into service of larger, more fuel-efficient freight carriers, such as the DC-10, the MD-11, and the Boeing 747, and with advances in logistics.

Third, the growth of trade was boosted by the offshoring of manufacturing from the European countries, Japan, and the United States to industrializing economies, where wages, rents, and other costs were lower. Major retailers in the United States took the lead,[8] followed by manufacturers, lured by the profits to be earned from shifting production overseas. An international production system began to take shape, initially under the tutelage of multinational corporations (MNCs), but increasingly, this system was complemented by the rise of Asian contract manufacturers, such as Flextronics and Hon Hai, and integrators, among which Li & Fung is the most prominent.

Fourth, the initial round of production offshoring and outsourcing to suppliers in emerging economies was followed by a far-reaching elaboration, specialization, and geographic dispersion of production, made possible by growing expertise in managing complex manufacturing and product integration processes, the profits to be earned by extending the value chains, and the greater ease of doing so with the help of newly devised information technologies. Induced by the trade rounds referred to earlier, a series of technological, institutional, networking, and process-related advances that stimulated trade ushered in a new era of globalization that was arguably more inclusive and prosperous than the globalization of the early 20th century.

There were four additional facets to the globalizing trend starting in the 1980s. One, already alluded to, was financial globalization, which arose from the loosening of capital controls, as well as from financial innovations and institutional developments that increased the salience of the banking and finance sector in the advanced countries and encouraged their banks and finance houses to join manufacturing firms in seeking opportunities overseas. Finance, like water once it begins to flow and spread, is difficult to keep out, and spread it did, as the industry acquired a voice (particularly in the United Kingdom and United States), mobilized political support, and began making the case that rapid development was predicated on easier access to an elastic supply of international capital and to financial instruments that differed according to the varying needs of savers and investors.[9] The integration of financial markets, which triggered the flow of

---

[8]Major retailers in the United States are among the largest importers, and as the retail sector has become more concentrated since the mid 1990s, imports from industrializing countries such as China and Mexico have soared (Basker and Van 2010).

[9]The contribution of financial development to growth is supported by empirical research reviewed by Demirgüç-Kunt and Levine (2008) and Levine (2005). Aghion, Fally, and Scarpetta (2007) underscore the role of finance in supporting the entry and growth of firms, and Philippon and Véron (2008) show that access to financing can significantly influence the appearance and the fortunes of high-tech manufacturing and services providers.

portfolio finance, coincided with the growth of foreign direct investment (FDI) from US$56 billion in 1985 to US$343 billion in 1995 and US$955 billion in 2005 (United Nations Global Compact 2006).

A second facet was the deepening of manufacturing capabilities in a number of developing countries. Once concentrated in a few advanced economies, modern manufacturing activities began striking roots in many more economies helped by the multiplication and deepening of trade channels, the nuclei for industrialization created by FDI, and the spread of international value chains.

The third facet of globalization of relevance to the Sifire story is the coalescence of trading blocs, which began generating their own virtuous spirals through greater interdependency and intraregional and intraindustry trade. By helping meld most of the European economies into a single market with its own currency and increasingly uniform standards and regulations, the European Union (EU) magnified the benefits inherent in integration for the participating countries (Barysch 2004). In addition to the gains to be realized from globalization, the European economies enlarged the continentwide benefits by creating a market of more than half a billion consumers. Other regional and bilateral trading arrangements also proliferated after the 1980s,[10] notably in East Asia, and although their incremental contribution to the ongoing multilateral changes is debated, on balance they did not undermine globalization. They may very well have helped open a few doors and thickened the incentives for firms engaging in cross-border activities or considering such activities.

Globalization's fourth significant facet is the diffusion of general-purpose technologies (GPTs).[11] The role of technology differentiates this second round of global integration from the first. GPTs such as electricity and the internal combustion engine began spurring innovations in the late 19th and early 20th centuries, but it would be fair to say that their significant effects were felt in the decades following World War I.[12] Lower transport costs, made possible by steam-driven ships certainly shaved transport costs,[13] but GPTs were not the force behind the first

---

[10]As of May 15, 2011, the World Trade Organization had received notification of 489 regional trade agreements. See http://www.wto.org/english/tratop_e/region_e/region_e.htm.

[11]GPTs are distinguished by their potential for evolution, applicability across a wide range of uses in numerous products and processes, and complementarities with existing or emerging technologies. See Brynjolfsson and Saunders (2010, 95).

[12]Electricity, the internal combustion engine, communication technologies, and new materials that shaped the 20th century first made an appearance in the latter part of the 19th century, but the full harnessing and growth these innovations generated filtered through several decades, extending well into the 20th century (Hummels 2007; Smil 2005).

[13]James (2009) links the era of globalization extending from the 1880s until the eve of World War I to the momentum imparted by the iron and steel industry and the revolution in transport resulting from steam-based power and iron-hulled ships with screw propellers (see Temin 1999).

globalization. The second globalization has undoubtedly benefited from the spate of technological advances unleashed by the semiconductor and the Internet, in addition to the continuing innovations arising from earlier GPTs, which are by no means a spent force. Computers, other electronic and telecommunication devices, and digital technologies have penetrated virtually every corner of the economy, and the presence of the Internet is pervasive. These GPTs are responsible for twin revolutions in manufacturing and in services. And these revolutions have had global consequences. The nature of the technologies has facilitated the dispersal of manufacturing, most notably in East Asia, through standardization and modularization of products and intermediates and the codification of production techniques. The twin revolutions have made possible the outsourcing and offshoring of impersonal services, thereby enabling countries such as India to build entirely new and thriving services sectors specializing in business process outsourcing, information technology–enabled services, and software that barely existed before 1990. The Internet and the web have also raised networking to an entirely new plane. Networking is as old as human society, but as currently practiced, thanks to advances in information technology (IT), it has become a major force driving change (Rennie and Zorpette 2011).[14]

GPTs lent impetus to the industrial miracles in East Asia, for example, and without them it would be difficult to imagine that international value chains could have evolved to the extent they have and that logistics and supply-chain management could ever have reached such a level of sophistication and productive efficiency. By harnessing the potential of the GPTs, countries were able to maximize the returns from other elements of globalization. Countries that became efficient producers of manufactures or proved adept at exploiting the Internet and digital technologies, enlarged the gains from trade, attracted more capital, and reaped lasting economic gains.

---

[14]Lucky (2000, 260, 262) believes that the new IT is much more potent than the telegraph and the telephone and is affecting the pace of science more decisively. To illustrate the point, he observes that although the solar eclipse that proved Albert Einstein's conjectures was observed on May 29, 1919, "Einstein had still not heard of the results as late as September 2nd. Then on September 27th, he received a telegram from Hendrik Lorentz informing him that Arthur Eddington had found the predicted displacement of starlight." Lucky points out that the telegraph, the telephone, and the wireless were all one-to-one topologies connecting two users. Radio and television are one-to-many topologies that broadcast to a great many users. The power of the new media derives from their "many to many" topologies. "They allow the sharing of information in textual, graphic, and multimedia formats across these communities, and they empower users within these communities to build their own applications. It is this empowerment of the periphery that has opened the floodgates of innovation to millions. . . . The key idea of the Internet—a simple, common core protocol with the intelligence at the periphery—was the critical ingredient of the culture from which the Internet arose."

The remarkable productivity of the GPTs, their ubiquity, and their dispersion across the world take us to the fifth facet of globalization, which is the role of ideas—their production and their rapid as well as widespread dissemination through the many channels created by IT-induced networking. The first round of globalization also drew some of its energy from the production and circulation of ideas on trade, technology, and political systems. In contrast, the ongoing globalization might never have achieved its current tempo had a substantial deepening of learning economies not occurred in Europe and the United States before World War II.[15] The massive expansion of these learning economies in the postwar decades and their effectiveness in generating ideas, some of which struck commercial roots, gave rise to new markets and triggered the emergence of companies that supplied these markets. Investment in education at all levels and in research within specialized institutions[16] and in the business sector,[17] coupled with the successful cultivation of a culture of innovation, produced a payoff that lifted growth rates in the second half of the 20th century and supported the gains in productivity that have increasingly sustained them since.

It is important to recognize the multidimensional characteristics of technological change and innovation made possible by investment in systems of learning and research. The revolution caused by advances in semiconductors, electronics, and telecommunication technologies is widely associated with new products and the ways products are manufactured. Undoubtedly, these advances have contributed significantly to economic change, but product innovation was powerfully reinforced by numerous collaborative innovations in other areas—for example, in services, institutions, organizations, and habits and lifestyles. GPTs have proven to be an extraordinarily potent transformative force because the learning economy generated a cross-disciplinary matrix of supporting and intersecting innovations that enormously magnified the influence of the core technologies.

Globalization, with some assistance from these very same GPTs, is a vehicle for disseminating ideas and technologies to countries that built modern learning and innovation systems capitalizing on the new opportunities much faster than the laggards. Globalization has promoted innovation by opening national systems and mobilizing talent from throughout the world to refine and extend existing

---

[15]Goldin and Katz (2009) attribute the great advances of the U.S. economy in the 20th century to the spread of schooling after 1910 and the further boost to education in the immediate decades after World War II.

[16]Such research received an enormous boost during World War II and the Cold War that followed from spending on research for military purposes, especially in the United States. See Markusen and others (1991) on military industrialization in the United States and Singer (2009) on defense-related technologies.

[17]Following Thomas Edison's lead (and that of German companies), large U.S. firms, notably in the chemicals industry, began creating research labs early in the 20th century.

technologies and to develop new technologies. This globalization of innovation activities[18] is a vital step, because the continuous deepening of knowledge in every field is demanding even greater specialization from researchers (with increasing investment of time). Advances in science and technology that require the pooling of expertise drawn from several subdisciplines necessarily involve the labor of teams made up of a number of specialists, and over time, the size of teams grows. National systems of learning and innovation nurture these specializations, but it is globalization that has spurred networking and collaboration by encouraging both face-to-face and electronic interaction among specialists; by giving birth to virtual communities of researchers; by making innovation a global enterprise that, bolstered by an array of publishing activities, straddles disciplines; and by supporting channels permitting the exchange and circulation of ideas or research results. Globalization facilitates faster technological catch-up and the building of production capabilities, and it can stimulate innovation if countries invest in the knowledge infrastructure to absorb ideas and technologies and engage in their further development.

Globalization powerfully affected the fortunes of late developers by supplying some of the scaffolding for the economic renaissance in Finland, Ireland, and Singapore. Absent global integration along the lines previously described and the incentives and pressures such globalization generated, it is difficult to imagine how these small countries could have squeezed so much economic transformation into less than two decades. Globalization, however, was an enabling element, albeit a major one. Other countries were equally well positioned to move forward but did not, which is what makes the Sifire experience so eminently instructive.

Old Light

For each of the Sifire countries, the most exciting and formative period extended from the mid 1980s through the 1990s, but some of the preconditions of later development must be sought in the two preceding decades. Three deserve the most attention. One was a process of consensus building among the key stakeholders—the government, the business community, and labor—regarding development objectives for small countries with limited natural resources. This complex process of aligning the objectives and winning the commitment of stakeholders was resolved in Singapore by the early 1970s. The political economy of development was on a firm footing in Finland, also by the mid-1970s, in part because virtually all members of the Finnish Parliament were engaged in discussing and determining economic policy programs (Dahlman, Routti, and Ylä-Anttila 2006).

---

[18]For more on the globalization of innovation, see Athreye and Cantwell (2007); Athukorala and Kohpaiboon (2010); Carlsson (2006); Jaruzelski and Dehoff (2008); Lewin and Couto (2007).

Ireland, however, took longer to arrive at a workable understanding of how to pursue development. A start was made in the 1950s with the partial abandonment of the protectionist policies adopted after 1932, which had begun stifling growth and employment generation,[19] and the process continued in the 1960s when investment in education won political favor. Support for European Economic Community (EEC) membership helped push the cause of export-led economic modernization, an interest that was aroused in the late 1950s following the publication of Albert Hirschman's (1958) influential *The Strategy of Economic Development*.[20] But for three decades thereafter, progress was slow because of the persistence of entrenched attitudes and vested interests, particularly those of rural property owners (Girvin 2010). It was not until the latter part of the 1980s that Charles Haughey managed to arrive at a durable agreement with all social partners on the management of the economy, a program for maintaining social stability, and a rebranding of Ireland as a country that was hospitable to MNCs and was moving away from narrow nationalism and Roman Catholicism toward a more progressive culture (Foster 2008). Consensus building in those earlier years created the understanding and social capital[21] for constructive political interaction and economic management.[22] The rules of the game for all parties were hammered out and gradually internalized, a process that helped to strengthen the sinews of administrative capabilities in the public sector and to contain uncertainties for decision makers in the business community, local as well as foreign. Each country tested the mechanisms for achieving political and macroeconomic stability and bestowed on them a degree of legitimacy.

A second precondition was the priority given to education and, in particular, to its quality. Of course, the level of commitment varied among the three countries, but the need for sound primary and secondary general education and the advantages of imparting vocational training to a fraction of the workforce were understood in all, with Finland and Singapore being the most committed. Early on, decision makers recognized the role of human resources in developing these

---

[19]See Durkan (2010) on the genesis of protectionism in the 1930s and the move toward openness. The Irish Export Board was founded in 1952.

[20]Hirschman's persuasive case for export industries that could lead through backward and forward links to a quickening of development and employment generation caught the attention of Seán Lemass and T. K. Whitaker, who, with the assistance of Louden Ryan, were responsible for guiding Ireland's industrial policy in the 1950s (Walsh and Whelan 2010).

[21]Ireland has traditionally been a tightly knit society with dense links facilitating the diffusion of social knowledge. Social capital can help bolster collective action, which is often undersupplied.

[22]Mac Sharry and White (2001) refer to the social partnership between the various interest groups in Ireland that helped resolve the fiscal crisis. This very same compact produced the consensus behind the opening of the economy, the joining of the EU, and the commitment to Europeanization (see also O'Toole 2009).

economies and planned accordingly. The future contribution of tertiary education was also perceived by the late 1980s as a means of supplying higher-order skills for a modern economy, and resources were channeled into expanding existing facilities and creating new ones.

A history of industrialization, however modest, was a third precondition. Without it, a country will struggle to accelerate growth, irrespective of the opportunities presented by external development and domestic shocks. The bar need not be set too high. Industrial capabilities in Finland, Ireland, and Singapore were fairly modest in the 1960s and the 1970s, and the base of manufacturing was narrow, but all three countries had been exposed to modern industrial practices by their proximity to major industrial nations and through indigenous manufacturing activities and trade. Moreover, Singapore was an important logistics hub and a former British naval base, with extensive repair and support facilities that served to embed engineering and metalworking skills.

Thus, rapid development in Sifire was preceded by

- The gradual articulation of a consensus on economic direction, leading to the development of political institutions for engaging stakeholders and resolving differences. Hence, the countries could maintain economic focus.
- Investment in the education system to provide universal primary education, to expand the coverage of secondary and vocational schooling, to raise quality standards, and to expand the tertiary-level knowledge economy.
- An accumulation of modern industrial capabilities in the late 1960s and 1970s.

There is no sound empirical basis for specifying preconditions appropriate for triggering rapid development in any one country or set of countries sharing broadly similar characteristics. And the three preconditions described earlier need not have sufficed. Success was the outcome of several additional factors, none of which was sufficient in itself, although in these three countries, the combination of factors proved to be a viable mix.

Crises and Consequences

Whether it is countries or companies that are affected, a crisis can catalyze a chain of decisions and changes with potentially far-reaching consequences. New leadership with a compelling vision that galvanizes reforms, removes bottlenecks, and triggers a round of investment is one outcome. A crisis by driving home the seriousness of the situation confronting a country—or a corporation—can also lead to the articulation of a longer-range strategy and the commitment to its systematic implementation by mobilizing existing institutions and organizations or by establishing new ones with an eye to the proposed strategy. Of course, not all crises lead to fruitful outcomes. Crises can result in panic, confusion, acrimonious political bickering, and ill-conceived decisions; a decline in the quality of governance; and the derailing of good long-term strategies. Indeed, though crises can present opportunities, seizing those opportunities is conditional on having certain capabilities in place, on possessing policy-making skills, on successfully assembling coalitions to back and implement new initiatives, and on establishing a fund of political goodwill that allows contending parties to bury their differences and overcome resistance from entrenched interests whose rents are threatened. In addition, every country can use a dose of luck.

During the 1980s and the 1990s, Ireland, Finland, and Singapore faced and responded to crises in ways that stimulated development. In the mid 1980s, Singapore realized that with domestic labor costs rising and competition mounting from other Southeast Asian economies, the low-cost assembly and processing model of industrialization would be unable to deliver the growth rates the city-state was seeking. A drastic slowing of the economy in the mid 1980s convinced the authorities of the need to contain the spiraling costs and, at the same time, begin switching tracks by diversifying into new products and services and upgrading existing activities.[23] A severe fiscal crisis starting in the late 1980s—the result of political mismanagement—forced Ireland to adopt the Tallaght Strategy[24] in 1987. The changes adopted would eventually enable Ireland, with the help of MNCs and its EU partners, to transition to a higher growth path. Finland was compelled to engage in bank restructuring and scramble for an alternative growth model following a severe financial crisis, which erupted in 1990, and the collapse of its principal export markets in the Soviet Union and Eastern European countries (see Honkapohja and others 2009). In short order, Finland needed to reduce its reliance on resource-based products and to groom new leading sectors with long-run potential in European and global markets.

Each of the countries had already established mechanisms for managing development—a process had begun in the 1960s in most countries, including some of the most backward, and was still ongoing. But for Sifire, the crises induced an overhaul and focusing of these mechanisms in three important respects. First, the advantages of defining a development path through a consultative process became more apparent. Crises helped crystallize options and prod decision makers to choose among alternatives by systematically gathering and evaluating data and by canvassing the views of market participants.

Second, the crises highlighted the desirability of mechanisms to reduce investment risks for domestic and foreign investors and thereby raise the level of investment through better coordination of the decisions of key players, of public investments, and of policy incentives. A development strategy was only a first step to be followed by others: mobilizing investor sentiment behind the strategy

---

[23]Singapore's industrial diversification and development of core technologies is graphed by Felipe (2010) using the product space technique pioneered by Hidalgo and Hausmann (2008).

[24]The strategy included tax, welfare, and competition reforms.

appeared to require extramarket institutions for achieving a degree of synchronicity, with a government agency acting as a convener, a clearinghouse for proposals, and a source of financing, as well as a source of signals to help orchestrate business decisions.[25]

The effectiveness of a long-term strategy and of coordinating mechanisms rested on a third factor, which was the governments' capacity to implement decisions, to follow through with promises, and to ensure that incentives were actually delivered with the minimum of transaction costs. Crises in these small economies underlined the advantages of public organizations with a limited number of clear objectives, a readiness to engage with key stakeholders, streamlined structures with few layers, and strict accountability.[26]

The lessons emerging from the 1980s that the three countries variously put into practice point to the following: (a) the valuable guidance that can be provided by a development strategy and institutions for consultation and coordination, (b) the advantages of enhancing policy implementation capabilities through organizational reforms and simplification of procedures,[27] and (c) the reduction of transaction costs weighing on the business community. The now ubiquitous "one-stop agency" was born.

Investing in Growth

Effective coordination with a follow-through of policies can induce the level of public and private investment in productive assets that is a significant source of growth directly through embodied technical progress and learning by doing. It was apparent in the 1980s that the growth rates Sifire sought hinged on a sufficient volume of domestic and foreign investment. Governments in each of the countries worked closely with the business community to build a competitive policy environment and to channel resources into industry. Finland's strategies and incentive policies focused on the domestic business sector, because the country had indigenous industrial capabilities and could build on them. Neither Ireland or Singapore had such capacities. To deepen the industrial system and move up the value chain in manufacturing and services, both countries required the foreign investment and technologies that only MNCs could provide. Ireland lacked domestic growth engines; Singapore had few, but most were publicly owned. Hence, development strategy, governance, and policy implementation were

---

[25]Such a role to compensate for the myopia and failures of the market has received much attention from Rodrik (2005) and earlier in the East Asian context from Amsden (1989, 2007); Amsden and Chu (2003); and Wade (1990).

[26]See Mader, Myers, and Kelman (2009) on government efficiency.

[27]This kind of streamlining is the hallmark of the Doing Business Indicators, Investment Climate Assessments, and Benchmarks of Competitiveness.

deliberately designed to attract MNCs that would provide ready-made jobs and growth and, over time, spillovers to stimulate local firms and promote start-up activities.[28] Both countries offered foreign investors a full suite of incentives. In addition, they engaged in intensive international marketing campaigns, seeking potential investors to ascertain their requirements and doing their utmost to meet those requirements through domestic investment in training, infrastructure, urban services, and amenities to attract private capital.

All three countries recognized the importance of investment in manufacturing by medium-size and large firms because those firms create better-paid jobs and benefit from scale economies, access to global markets, and the capacity to conduct research and development (R&D).[29] This two-pronged approach of incentivizing private investment, both domestic and foreign, and buttressing it with public investment worked well in Sifire. Governments also catered to new entrants and smaller firms in the interests of a dynamic churning of the industrial sector.[30] Also, new entrants are not infrequently the vehicles for introducing disruptive, often low-cost technologies that larger firms are inclined to shun, but once these technologies are proven, large firms embrace, improve, scale up, and market them.

Singapore's investment policy resulted in much higher rates of capital spending than is found in either Finland or Ireland. Its large government-linked corporations were more responsive to incentives, and longer-term financing was more readily available from public banking institutions and sovereign wealth funds. Singapore also succeeded in attracting a substantial flow of foreign capital into manufacturing. To burnish the country's attractiveness to foreign companies, the state spent lavishly on urban, transport, and communication infrastructure and on industrial parks.

EU structural funds[31] enabled Ireland to ramp up spending on infrastructure and education services, for example, and to partially offset the shortfall in

---

[28]MNCs provided an avenue for integrating local networks of indigenous firms with global corporate networks. This process of global integration is embedded, in O'Riain's (2000, 158) words, "in a set of neo-corporatist institutions that have managed the relation to the global economy of both the macro-economy and of unionized workers [in Ireland]."

[29]The important role of medium-size and large transnational firms from emerging economies is apparent from Aguiar and others (2009) and Verma and others (2011).

[30]A churning resulting in a turnover and replacement of firms throughout the food chain differentiates the U.S. economy from Japan's, which has maintained a relatively stable hierarchy of firms for decades. These entrenched behemoths have relied heavily on the domestic market for the sale of consumer electronics and computers and have seen their market share erode in overseas markets since the mid 2000s.

[31]After joining the EEC in 1973, Ireland received €17 billion from the EEC's (now EU's) structural funds between 1978 to 2003. These amounts may have added 0.5 percent yearly to the growth of gross domestic product in the 1990s (UNIDO 2005, 78). These structural funds, which were created to support the EU's regional development policy, were the European Regional Development Fund and the European Social Fund.

infrastructure spending between 1980 and the early 1990s,[32] but investment never soared to the levels reached in Singapore. Smaller flows of FDI to Ireland might also be linked to a focus on software and services rather than on hardware, although Dell, Intel, Fujitsu, Hewlett-Packard, and other electronics heavy-weights, mostly from the United States, did set up production units in Ireland.[33]

Finland's investment rate was comparable to Ireland's, although it pulled in much less FDI. As a consequence, growth never rose to the levels seen in Singapore and briefly in Ireland. In contrast to Singapore, Finland and Ireland were able to promote more domestic entrepreneurial activity and new entry, resulting in siz-able and vibrant pools of small and medium-size enterprises, a point that will be discussed later. However, in all three countries, much of the economic weight was concentrated in large corporations, both domestic and foreign.

Learning and Innovation

Countries respond to crises in different ways. Many turn to short-term fixes that frequently fail to correct systemic weaknesses and eliminate deep-seated distortions. A minority are prompted to take a hard and critical look at their economic fundamentals, to try to break away from a past trajectory, and to chart a new course. Finland, Ireland, and Singapore are among the countries that were able to take a longer view after a crisis and reorient their strategies.

By the 1980s, it was becoming apparent that by betting on the technologically dynamic industrial subsectors—principally electronics, telecommunications, chemicals, and pharmaceuticals—small countries could improve their longer-term growth prospects. Technological expertise was not a substitute for capital. Instead, it could multiply the returns from capital spending through heightened productivity and innovation. Making technology into a primary driver of the economy called for raising the capabilities of all segments of the workforce, from factory workers to managers to researchers and professionals of all stripes—what

---

[32]Investment in telecom facilities was sufficient and facilitated IT-based development in the 1990s.

[33]"A relatively low-cost, young, well-educated Irish labor force combined with a 10 percent tax rate—the lowest manufacturing tax rate in Europe and about one-third of that in the U.S.—has been attracting multinational manufacturers to Ireland for some time. . . . In 1996, IBM opened its European strategic operating site in Ireland, a $350m investment. Other major [original equipment manufacturers], including Dell Computer, Hewlett-Packard, Microsoft, and 3Com, have major operations in Ireland. Intel also has roots there, opening its first 0.25 nanometer microprocessor facility serving Europe" (Cornell 2001). UNIDO (2005, 80) observes that "inward FDI was greatly stimulated by Irish tax policy, the more so once Ireland was within the EU. [American companies have also been attracted by] agglomeration benefits . . . knowledge spillovers and thick labor markets."

might be described as an *O-ring approach*.[34] With the complexity of production techniques rising through the 1990s and IT infiltrating the workplace, maximizing manufacturing productivity demanded larger inputs of hard and soft skills.[35] The quality of management was correlated with technology adoption, efficient resource use, incremental innovation, and human resource development (Bloom and others 2010). Better-educated individuals were more likely to engage in entrepreneurial activity and to start up high-tech activities (Berry and Glaeser 2005). They also hired more skilled workers and favored research. Investment in tertiary and vocational education increased the porosity of an economy to the latest technologies and nudged it closer to the production frontier. More important, this process of absorption and the concomitant closing of technology gaps strengthened the case for domestic R&D and encouraged technology deepening, not just in narrowly defined scientific fields, but more generally through innovation across the board in, for example, organization, marketing, health services, and teaching.

In embracing technology as a driver of long-term growth, Sifire successfully engaged in building capabilities. This success is the core of the Sifire model and resulted in the making of a networked learning and innovation system (LIS) of the front rank. Finland and Singapore, if not Ireland, can claim to have created world-class systems.

The foundation of a world-class system comprises universal primary and secondary education with high quality standards. Some research suggests that the quality of secondary school students measured by international test scores such as TIMSS (Trends in International Mathematics and Science Study) and PISA (Programme for International Student Assessment) are among the more significant determinants of growth (see chapter 3) (Hanushek and Kimko 2000). Allied with vocational training for those who do not enter secondary school or do not earn higher degrees, this grounding in quality education and

---

[34]The O-ring theory of economic development was popularized by Kremer (1993), who based it on the failure of a small rubber seal, which Richard Feynman dramatically identified as the culprit in the Challenger space shuttle disaster in 1986.

[35]Technology development has been geared to the factor and skill endowments of advanced countries, and research has pointed to a skill bias (see Acemoğlu 1998; Acemoğlu and Zilibotti 2001; Caselli 1999). The rapid catch-up by Sifire was facilitated by a buildup of skills to extract the maximum productivity advantage from the latest technologies and to create the capacity to tweak and extend these technologies through indigenous innovation. The diffusion of information and communication technologies and the increased share of IT-based capital investment have served to increase the demand for highly skilled workers as against those with midrange skills (Michaels, Natraj, and van Reenen 2010). Moreover, the bias of technological change overall appears to favor the substitution of capital and digital technologies for labor and jobs for the most skilled over jobs for those with a modest level of skills (Brynjolfsson and McAfee 2011).

training is the basis for a competitive learning economy and preparation for tertiary-level training.

Since the 1980s, the increasing skill bias of technology and the displacement of midlevel white-collar workers engaged in routine tasks by IT have meant that to find employment many more technical and white-collar workers need tertiary-level qualifications, with a higher percentage of researchers requiring doctoral degrees (Autor and Dorn 2011; Michaels, Natraj, and van Reenen 2010). The Sifire strategies anticipated the demand for such higher-level skills—especially science, technology, engineering, and mathematic (STEM) skills—to achieve competitiveness in technology-intensive activities. The countries moved quickly to begin expanding the capacity and quality of universities, although achieving both outcomes could take many years. Priority was also given to research capacity in selected universities, with a focus on science and engineering disciplines. All three countries put a premium on math and science skills at the high school and college levels in anticipation of future demand from the activities that were to comprise the backbone of the economies.

Policy makers in Sifire were conscious that an LIS needed to work with and cater to the productive sectors and contribute to their competitiveness. Doing so meant fulfilling three requirements. First, teaching institutions and vocational schools had to be sensitive to market signals regarding types of skills in demand and had to ensure that their graduates cleared the bar of quality. To satisfy businesses and other employers, universities needed employers' inputs and support when designing curricula and course offerings and in complementing these courses with faculty staffing, internship arrangements, scholarship support, and postdoctoral positions. Creating effective feedback loops between the university sector and the business community was a major hurdle, and surmounting it was facilitated by the intermediation of key government agencies.[36] Such coordination and feedback are widely accepted as a necessary objective, but one that often proves elusive. The Sifire strategy came closer to obtaining the sought-after results and minimizing the mismatching of skills.

Second, the research universities needed to become a fruitful source of ideas, of interdisciplinary capabilities, and of some patentable technologies of commercial value that would lead to local start-ups. Academia was never assumed to be the principal source of ready-to-market technologies. It would train researchers and engage in basic research, thereby adding to the fund of usable knowledge. Also, academia would devote some resources to upstream applied research financed by its own resources, government funding, and contractual arrangements with firms. University-industry links that led to a circulation of knowledge and researchers

---

[36]With 20 universities, Finland's planned higher education system enjoys limited autonomy and staffing. The courses offered are strongly influenced by forecasts of labor market demand, very much along the lines followed by Singapore (OECD 2007).

and a flow of financing to universities were a significant ingredient of the strategy. Furthermore, universities were viewed as a source of entrepreneurship to help transfer innovation to the business sector.[37]

The LIS saw universities playing a vital supporting role with businesses, especially the large firms doing the bulk of the applied research and commercial innovation. In Ireland and Singapore, the focus of development agencies and education institutions was initially on serving the MNCs. In Finland, Nokia took the lead, in conjunction with the National Board of Education, the Ministry of Education, and the Future Committee of the Parliament, in persuading the Academy of Finland to accelerate the initiative to become a knowledge society by mobilizing universities and public research entities (OECD 2007).[38] In other words, these small economies adopted a business-first learning and innovation strategy.

Third, in building a world-class LIS, small economies must accept a high degree of openness[39] and be ready to compete with the best—or risk losing their most talented people.[40] The experience of Sifire puts the spotlight on an important lesson, which is the need to set high standards for an LIS and to adopt international pay scales to ensure that the LIS is "sticky" and avoids a net loss of the best minds. High standards come at a price; they entail building a costly infrastructure of libraries, lab facilities, and office space and staffing universities with qualified and expensive employees able to impart state-of-the-art knowledge.[41] The top echelon of knowledge workers have seen global opportunities multiply and, as a result, are exceedingly mobile. Their home-country bias is frequently outweighed by the package of incentives and the quality of the working and living conditions that are to their satisfaction. In addition to university and research facilities, "stickiness" is a function of two other elements of the LIS. First is the dynamism of the business sector, its offer of technological challenges, and its commitment to competing on the basis of innovation. Second is the creativity of the urban environment. Ireland and Singapore have relied on high-tech MNCs

---

[37]MIT and Stanford were the prototypical entrepreneurial universities, and they remain the leaders all others seek to emulate. See, for instance, Etzkowitz (2002); Kaiser (2010); Lecuyer (2006); Lenoir and others (2005); and Leslie and Kargon (2006).

[38]This effort was broadened in 2000, with the Academy acting in tandem with Tekes (the Finnish Funding Agency for Technology and Innovation), other agencies, and the University of Helsinki to push interdisciplinary research, partnerships, and lifelong learning.

[39]See Alesina and Wacziarg (1997). Countries with populations of less than a million average a ratio of imports to gross domestic product of 60 percent, three times the ratio for developing countries in general.

[40]Ireland suffered from a continuing drain of workers that was reversed only in the mid 1990s.

[41]See the papers on the making of world-class universities in Altbach and Salmi (2011).

and international services providers to craft a suitably attractive technological ambience.[42] Finland has depended more on home-grown companies, most notably Nokia,[43] and start-ups that have demonstrated international competitiveness.

Creative Cities

All three countries have worked hard at improving their urban environments so as to make them more appealing to footloose knowledge workers.[44] The weather does not favor Dublin,[45] Helsinki, or Singapore, but each has had some success in acquiring the cachet of a creative city and an innovative hotspot. Helsinki is the Design Capital of 2012 and Turku is one of the European Capitals of Culture 2011. Investment in urban transport, good-quality housing, recreational amenities, services and security, connectivity, and cultural activities has helped put these cities on the map. Finland's Centers of Expertise Program, launched in 1994, was the start of a continuing regional policy to increase the competitiveness of its cities. Singapore has made a name for itself as an air-conditioned city (George 2000). And because innovative activities and virtually all manufacturing and services are concentrated in relatively few urban areas, urban design, livability, and attractiveness are intrinsic to the success of an LIS. This need was not as apparent in the 1980s, but with globalization and brain circulation, the quality of cities is a central thread of an LIS and is seen as such by Sifire.

Information and communication technologies (ICTs) are the GPTs responsible for much of the huge burst of innovation during the past three decades. Early in the game, Sifire perceived the potential and began designing strategies accordingly to seize opportunities as they arose. Computer literacy and, more generally, IT readiness were among the objectives given prominence in equipping the workforce. They have yielded rich dividends. First, Sifire targeted the development of ICT-based industries and, through domestic and foreign investment, built the production base that has been a major source of growth, of gains in productivity, and of diversification. Second, by taking the lead in building an ICT infrastructure

---

[42]Both countries have had some success in creating a stable of home-grown companies. Irish firms are well represented in industries such as agroprocessing and food, cosmetics, construction, packaging, and equipment manufacturing (O'Riain 2000). Singapore's banks, transportation companies such as Neptune, engineering companies such as and conglomerates such as Keppel Corporation now have international standing.

[43]The launch of a GSM (Global System for Mobile Communications) phone in 1992, the Nokia 1011, initiated Nokia's climb to the apex of the global telecommunication industry.

[44]Richard Florida (2005) and, more recently, Edward Glaeser (2011) have emphasized the growth potential and resilience of human capital–intensive knowledge cities. Others (including Glaeser) are drawing attention to the contribution such cities can make to the greening of the planet (Kahn 2010).

[45]In Dublin, at any time, it is either raining or rain is imminent.

and encouraging the assimilation of IT in a wide range of activities, these small economies have reaped significant returns. ICT has helped transform (and flatten) organizational structures, skill profiles, work routines, and modes of interaction and collaboration. It has also reduced transaction costs of business, simplified governance, and provided innovation opportunities across a multitude of industries, including health care (Atkinson and others 2010; Brynjolfsson and Saunders 2010). Other countries grasped the potential of ICT, but Sifire extracted greater mileage than most by integrating ICT into development strategies encompassing industrialization and a closely interlaced LIS. The potential of IT has become increasingly apparent to nations and firms, and most have moved to exploit such technologies with varying degrees of success. The largest productivity gains from learning and greater openness to ideas have accrued to countries that have made IT an integral component of ongoing development by making incremental changes in many different areas and by evaluating and making subsequent modifications in light of lengthening knowledge and the steady drizzle of innovations.

What Sifire Got Right

An upswing in global integration was apparent in the early 1980s, and a round of industrial change seemed to be in the offing, but it was hard to identify the likely winners among the middle- and lower-middle-income countries. Finland, Ireland, and Singapore were some of the contenders, but 30 years ago they did not strike observers as being the most advantaged. The three countries proved more adept than their competitors in anticipating and seizing opportunities. By augmenting human capital and intangible assets and by providing the framework for networking, they encouraged technological assimilation and innovation even as a cornucopia of discoveries associated with new GPTs created industrial niches for profitable new products and tradable services.

Globalization and the pace of technological change served as the enabling conditions for these countries—as they did for others as well—but Sifire's widening lead over other countries emerged from the forging of domestic consensus in support of long-term-development strategies that were keyed to the quality of human capital, intangible factors, and an open, productively networked system of innovation and learning. The focus on human capital committed these countries to building their education and training assets. The importance attached to intangibles and the soft infrastructure undergirding development meant that institutions and capabilities supporting planning, coordinated policy making, policy implementation, the evaluation of results, and the integrity of governance mechanisms were given due attention. In conjunction with public investment policies and the incentive regime, intangible capital and networks contained business uncertainties and promoted private investment.

The incentive regime and the quality of the infrastructure—hard and soft—proved to be a fertile environment for businesses. Major MNCs set up shop in Ireland and Singapore, and Finland was able to grow its own successful companies. Smaller firms also flourished in the two European countries and to a lesser extent in Singapore.

The capstone of this development strategy was the LIS, which through government intermediation and the cultivation of feedback loops helped to match the requirements of the business sector for varieties of human capital with the supply produced by education and training institutions. The feedback loops connecting the training with the business sectors communicated information on standards of education quality and the employment readiness of graduates needed to maintain industrial competitiveness. The LIS also served to optimize the level and distribution of R&D among the various entities conducting research and attempted to strike a balance among technology absorption, basic research, and the different categories of applied research and to arrive at workable arrangements for financing the research. Learning was assigned a central role in the development strategy in the interests of broad-ranging economic competitiveness, which was the surest path to growth. Innovation was seen as a valuable byproduct of a dynamic learning system that contributed tangibly to productivity and profitability.

References

Acemoğlu, Daron. 1998. "Why Do New Technologies Complement Skills? Directed Technical Change and Wage Inequality." *Quarterly Journal of Economics* 113 (4): 1055–89.

Acemoğlu, Daron, and Fabrizio Zilibotti. 2001. "Productivity Differences." *Quarterly Journal of Economics* 116 (2): 563–606.

Aghion, Philippe, Thibault Fally, and Stefano Scarpetta. 2007. "Credit Constraints as a Barrier to the Entry and Post-Entry Growth of Firms." IZA Discussion Paper 3237, Institute for the Study of Labor, Bonn, Germany.

Aguiar, Marcos, Cameron Bailey, Arindam Bhattacharya, Thomas Bradtke, Jesús de Juan, Jim Hemerling, Kim Wee Koh, David C. Michael, Harold L. Sirkin, Carl Stern, Andrew Tratz, Kevin Waddell, and Bernd Waltermann. 2009. "The 2009 BCG 100 New Global Challengers: How Companies from Rapidly Developing Economies Are Contending for Global Leadership." Boston Consulting Group, Boston. http://www.bcg.com/documents/file20519.pdf.

Alesina, Alberto, and Romain Wacziarg. 1997. "Openness, Country Size, and the Government." NBER Working Paper 6024, National Bureau of Economic Research, Cambridge, MA.

Altbach, Philip G., and Jamil Salmi, eds. 2011. *The Road to Academic Excellence: The Making of World-Class Research Universities.* Washington, DC: World Bank.

Amsden, Alice H. 1989. *Asia's Next Giant: South Korea and Late Industrialization.* New York: Oxford University Press.

———. 2007. *Escape from Empire: The Developing World's Journey through Heaven and Hell.* Cambridge, MA: MIT Press.

Amsden, Alice H., and Wan-wen Chu. 2003. *Beyond Late Development: Taiwan's Upgrading Policies.* Cambridge, MA: MIT Press.

Athreye, Suma, and John Cantwell. 2007. "Creating Competition? Globalisation and the Emergence of New Technology Producers." *Research Policy* 36 (2): 209–26.

Athukorala, Prema-chandra, and Archanun Kohpaiboon. 2010. "East Asia in World Trade: The Decoupling Fallacy, Crisis, and Policy Challenges." Departmental Working Paper 2010-05, Arndt-Corden Department of Economics, Australian National University, Canberra.

Atkinson, Robert D., Stephen J. Ezell, Scott M. Andes, Daniel D. Castro, and Richard Bennett. 2010. *The Internet Economy 25 Years after .Com: Transforming Commerce and Life.* Washington, DC: Information Technology and Innovation Foundation. http://www.itif.org/files/2010-25-years.pdf.

Autor, David, and David Dorn. 2011. "The Growth of Low-Skill Service Jobs and the Polarization of the U.S. Labor Market." Working Paper, Massachusetts Institute of Technology, Cambridge, MA.

Barysch, Katinka. 2004. "EU Enlargement: How to Reap the Benefits." *Economic Trends* 2: 28–31. http://www.cer.org.uk/pdf/barysch_economictrends_june%2004.pdf.

Basker, Emek, and Pham Hoang Van. 2010. "Imports 'Я' Us: Retail Chains as Platforms for Developing-Country Imports. *American Economic Review* 100 (2): 414–18.

Beaulier, Scott A. 2003. "Explaining Botswana's Success: The Critical Role of Post-colonial Policy." *Cato Journal* 23 (2): 227–40. http://www.cato.org/pubs/journal/cj23n2/cj23n2-6.pdf.

Berry, Christopher R., and Edward L. Glaeser. 2005. "The Divergence of Human Capital Levels across Cities." HIER Discussion Paper 2091, Harvard Institute of Economic Research, Cambridge, MA.

Bloom, Nicholas, Aprajit Mahajan, David McKenzie, and John Roberts. 2010. "Why Do Firms in Developing Countries Have Low Productivity?" *American Economic Review* 100 (2): 619–23.

Bordo, Michael D., and Peter L. Rousseau. 2011. "Historical Evidence on the Finance-Trade-Growth Nexus." NBER Working Paper 17024, National Bureau of Economic Research, Cambridge, MA.

Brynjolfsson, Erik, and Andrew McAfee. 2011. *Race against the Machine: How the Digital Revolution Is Accelerating Innovation, Driving Productivity, and Irreversibly Transforming Employment and the Economy.* Lexington, MA: Digital Frontier Press.

Brynjolfsson, Erik, and Adam Saunders. 2010. *Wired for Innovation: How Information Technology Is Reshaping the Economy.* Cambridge, MA: MIT Press.

Carlsson, Bo. 2006. "Internationalization of Innovation Systems: A Survey of the Literature." *Research Policy* 35 (1): 56–67.

Caselli, Francesco. 1999. "Technological Revolutions." *American Economic Review* 89 (1): 78–102.

Cornell, Rhonda. 2001. "Ireland: Gateway to Europe." *Electronic Times*, January 15.

Dahlman, Carl J., Jorma Routti, and Pekka Ylä-Anttila. 2006. *Finland as a Knowledge Economy: Elements of Success and Lessons Learned.* Washington, DC: World Bank.

Demirgüç-Kunt, Asli, and Ross Levine. 2008. "Finance and Economic Opportunity." Policy Research Working Paper 4468, World Bank, Washington, DC.

Durkan, Joe. 2010. "Seán Lemass and the Nadir of Protectionism." *Economic and Social Review* 41 (3): 269–82. http://www.esr.ie/vol41_3/03-durkan.pdf.

Etzkowitz, Henry. 2002. *MIT and the Rise of Enterprenurial Science.* London: Routledge.

Felipe, Jesus. 2010. "Industrial Policy, Capabilities, and Growth: Where Does the Future of Singapore Lie?" Presentation at the Singapore Economic Policy Forum 2010, Singapore, October 22. http://www.cscollege.gov.sg/cpe/images/Jesus%20Felipe%20Industrial%20Policy%202.pdf.

Florida, Richard. 2005. *Cities and the Creative Class.* New York: Routledge.

Foster, Robert Fitzroy. 2008. *Luck and the Irish: A Brief History of Change from 1970.* Oxford, U.K.: Oxford University Press.

George, Cherian. 2000. *Singapore: The Air-Conditioned Nation—Essays on the Politics of Comfort and Control, 1990–2000.* Singapore: Landmark Books.

Girvin, Brian. 2010. "Before the Celtic Tiger: Change without Modernisation in Ireland 1959–1989." *Economic and Social Review* 41 (3): 349–65.

Glaeser, Edward L. 2011. *Triumph of the City: How Our Greatest Invention Makes Us Richer, Smarter, Greener, Happier, and Healthier.* New York: Penguin.

Goldin, Claudia, and Lawrence F. Katz. 2009. "The Race between Education and Technology: The Evolution of U.S. Educational Wage Differentials, 1890 to 2005." Harvard University and National Bureau of Economic Research, Cambridge, MA. http://www.economics.harvard.edu/faculty/katz/files/Chapter8_NBER_1.pdf.

Hanushek, Eric A., and Dennis D. Kimko. 2000. "Schooling, Labor Force Quality, and the Growth of Nations." *American Economic Review* 90 (5): 1184–208.

Hidalgo, César A., and Ricardo Hausmann. 2008. "A Network View of Economic Development." *Development Alternatives* 12 (1): 5–10. http://www.chidalgo.com/Papers/HidalgoHausmann_DAI_2008.pdf.

Hirschman, Albert O. 1958. *The Strategy of Economic Development.* New Haven, CT: Yale University Press.

Honkapohja, Seppo, Erkki A. Koskela, Willi Leibfritz, and Roope Uusitalo. 2009. *Economic Prosperity Recaptured: The Finnish Path from Crisis to Rapid Growth.* Cambridge, MA: MIT Press.

Hummels, David. 2007. "Transportation Costs and International Trade in the Second Era of Globalization." *Journal of Economic Perspectives* 21 (3): 131–54.

James, Harold. 2009. "The Late, Great Globalization." *Current History* 108 (714): 20–25.

Jaruzelski, Berry, and Kevin Dehoff. 2008. "Beyond Borders: The Global 1000." *Strategy and Business* 53 (winter).

Kahn, Matthew E. 2010. *Climatopolis: How Our Cities Will Thrive in the Hotter Future.* New York: Basic Books.

Kaiser, David, ed. 2010. *Becoming MIT: Moments of Decision.* Cambridge, MA: MIT Press.

Kremer, Michael. 1993. "O-Ring Theory of Economic Development." *Quarterly Journal of Economics* 108 (3): 551–75.

Lecuyer, Christophe. 2006. *Making Silicon Valley: Innovation and the Growth of High Tech, 1930–1970.* Cambridge, MA: MIT Press.

Lenoir, Timothy, Nathan Rosenberg, Henry Rowen, Christophe Lécuyer, Jeannette Colyvas, and Brent Goldfarb. 2005. "Inventing the Entrepreneurial University: Stanford and the Co-evolution of Silicon Valley." Stanford University, Stanford, CA.

Leslie, Stuart W., and Robert Kargon. 2006. "Exporting MIT: Science, Technology, and Nation-Building in India and Iran." *Osiris* 21 (1): 110–30.

Levine, Ross. 2005. "Finance and Growth: Theory and Evidence." In *Handbook of Economic Growth*, vol. 1A, ed. Philippe Aghion and Steven Durlauf, 865–934. Amsterdam: North-Holland.

Levinson, Marc. 2006. *The Box: How the Shipping Container Made the World Smaller and the World Economy Bigger.* Princeton, NJ: Princeton University Press.

Lewin, Arie Y., and Vinay Couto. 2007. *Next Generation Offshoring: The Globalization of Innovation.* Chicago: Booz Allen Hamilton. https://offshoring.fuqua.duke.edu/orn_report.pdf.

Lucky, Robert. 2000. "The Quickening of Science Communication." *Science* 289 (5477): 259–89.

Mac Sharry, Ray, and Padraic White. 2001. *The Making of the Celtic Tiger: The Inside Story of Ireland's Boom Economy.* Cork, Ireland: Mercier.

Mader, Dave, Jeff Myers, and Steven Kelman. 2009. "Overview of 'What It Takes to Change Government' Study." Booz Allen Hamilton, McLean, VA. http://www.boozallen.com/consulting/advance-our-government/what-it-takes-to-change-government/what-it-takes-to-change-government-overview.

Markusen, Ann, Peter Hall, Scott Campbell, and Sabina Deitrick. 1991. *The Rise of the Gunbelt.* New York: Oxford University Press.

Michaels, Guy, Ashwini Natraj, and John van Reenen. 2010. "Has ICT Polarized Skill Demand? Evidence from Eleven Countries over 25 Years." NBER Working Paper 16138, National Bureau of Economic Research, Cambridge, MA.

OECD (Organisation for Economic Co-operation and Development). 2007. *Higher Education and Regions: Globally Competitive, Locally Engaged.* OECD: Paris.

O'Riain, Seán. 2000. "The Flexible Developmental State: Globalization, Information Technology, and the 'Celtic Tiger.'" *Politics and Society* 28 (2): 157–93.

O'Toole, Fintan. 2009. *Ship of Fools: How Stupidity and Corruption Sank the Celtic Tiger.* London: Faber and Faber.

Philippon, Thomas, and Nicolas Véron. 2008. "Better Finance for More Enterprise Growth in Europe." VoxEU.org, February 22. http://www.voxeu.org/index.php?q=node/948.

Rennie, John, and Glenn Zorpette. 2011. "The Social Era of the Web Starts Now." *IEEE Spectrum*, June. http://spectrum.ieee.org/telecom/internet/the-social-era-of-the-web-starts-now.

Rodrik, Dani. 2005. "Growth Strategies." In *Handbook of Economic Growth*, ed. Philippe Aghion and Steven N. Durlauf, 967–1014. Amsterdam: North-Holland.

Singer, Peter W. 2009. *Wired for War: The Robotics Revolution and Conflict in the 21st Century.* New York: Penguin.

Smil, Vaclav. 2005. *Creating the Twentieth Century: Technical Innovations of 1867–1914 and Their Lasting Impact.* Oxford, U.K.: Oxford University Press.

———. 2010. *Prime Movers of Globalization: The History and Impact of Diesel Engines and Gas Turbines.* Cambridge, MA: MIT Press.

Temin, Peter. 1999. "Globalization." *Oxford Review of Economic Policy* 15 (4): 76–89.

UNIDO (United Nations Industrial Development Organization). 2005. *Industrial Development Report 2005: Capability Building for Catching-Up—Historical, Empirical, and Policy Dimensions.* Vienna, Austria: UNIDO.

United Nations Global Compact. 2006. "Global FDI Set to Surge Past US$1trn in 2006, Despite Fears of Backlash." United Nations Global Compact, New York. http://www.unglobalcompact.org/newsandevents/news_archives/2006_09_04.html.

Verma, Sharad, Kanika Sanghi, Holger Michaelis, Patrick Dupoux, Dinesh Khanna, and Philippe Peters. 2011. "Global Challengers: Companies on the Move—Rising Stars from Rapidly Developing Economies Are Reshaping Global Industries." Boston Consulting Group, Boston.

Wade, Robert. 1990. *Governing the Market: Economic Theory and the Role of the Government in East Asian Industrialization.* Princeton, NJ: Princeton University Press.

Walsh, Patrick Paul, and Ciara Whelan. 2010. "Hirschman and Irish Industrial Policy." *Economic and Social Review* 41 (3): 283–99. http://www.esr.ie/vol41_3/04-walsh.pdf.

3

Elements of a Learning Economy

Between 1970 and 2000, the economies of Singapore, Finland, and Ireland (Sifire) underwent dramatic changes. At the beginning of the period, they trailed the advanced economies by a wide margin and appeared handicapped by their smallness and lack of natural resources. However, within a matter of two decades, they had pulled abreast of the front-runners of the early 21st century. As noted in the previous chapters, these economies were able to catch two important economic waves in the latter half of the 20th century—the electronics and information technology (IT) revolutions and globalization—by adopting growth strategies that developed production geared toward exports of electronics, telecommunications, software, chemicals, and pharmaceuticals while continuing to sustain competitiveness in a number of traditional industries. In Ireland and Singapore, foreign direct investment (FDI) was the key driver of industrial change and exports. Finland relied less on FDI inflow than Ireland and Singapore. The performance of all three countries was crucially linked to the growth of regional and U.S. markets. Ireland and Finland benefited from the European Union (EU), and Singapore benefited from being a part of the fastest-growing region of the world.

All three economies anchored their growth strategies to the deepening of education. In the early stages, they focused on good primary and secondary education (including vocational education) to cater to expanding industrial sectors. From the late 1990s, as the three began approaching technology frontiers, tertiary education began receiving equal attention.

Changes in Economic Structure

The three Sifire countries started as resource-based and processing economies. In 1970, one-half of Finland's industrial output was from the food, textile, wood, and pulp and paper industries (see figure 3.1). By 2000, the shares of these four

Figure 3.1   Finland's Industrial Composition, 1970–2007

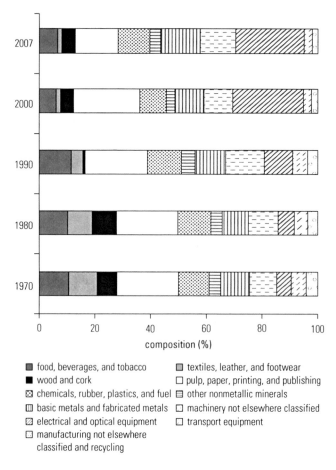

composition (%)

- ■ food, beverages, and tobacco
- ■ wood and cork
- ⊠ chemicals, rubber, plastics, and fuel
- ⊞ basic metals and fabricated metals
- ▨ electrical and optical equipment
- ☐ manufacturing not elsewhere classified and recycling
- ▨ textiles, leather, and footwear
- ☐ pulp, paper, printing, and publishing
- ⊟ other nonmetallic minerals
- ☐ machinery not elsewhere classified
- ☐ transport equipment

Source: United Nations Industrial Development Organization's INDSTAT3 database.

industrial subsectors had decreased to less than one-third and to about one-fourth of industrial production in 2007, largely because of the phenomenal growth of the information and communication technology (ICT) sector. However, the traditional industries remain vital to the economy, and firms such as Patria (military vehicles and defense hardware), KONE (elevators and escalators), Wärtsilä (marine engines and power-generating equipment), Neste Oil (fats and oils), UPM (pulp and paper), Huhtamaki (paper and packaging), Valio (dairy products), Amer Sports (garments), and Stora Enso (paper and cardboard), each with a turnover of more than €1 billion, are no less important than the ICT-based ones. Twenty-five companies account for half of all exports, and after Canada, Finland is the largest exporter of paper and cardboard. Electronics and electrical industries (including telecommunication equipment) began taking root in the 1960s, assisted by the links between technology-intensive producers of forest-based products and nascent engineering and electronics industries, with rapid growth occurring in the 1980s and 1990s (Dahlman, Routti, and Ylä-Anttila 2007).[1] By the late 1990s, electronics accounted for almost one-third of total exports (Saarinen 2005).

During the 1970s,[2] Ireland was still mainly an agricultural economy, one of the poorest in Europe.[3] Industrial activities were initially dominated by the food subsector, followed by the textile, wood, and pulp and paper sectors (see figure 3.2). Once the high-growth strategy gained traction in the 1980s, development was spearheaded by FDI in high-tech subsectors such as ICT, chemicals, and pharmaceuticals and by internationally traded services (Rios-Morales and Brennan 2009),[4] while domestic firms concentrated on traditional and food-processing industries (Barrios, Görg, and Strobl 2005).[5] As the involvement of multinational corporations (MNCs) expanded, so also did the industrial footprints of the ICT, pharmaceutical, and chemical subsectors. Nevertheless, Ireland's traditional strengths in the food-processing industries and construction materials are as important as those of Finland. Firms such as the Kerry Group (a leading supplier

---

[1]The telecom industry in Finland was relatively unregulated from the very beginning. The landline network was never monopolized by a national company, unlike in other countries. Also, free competition was allowed in the telecommunication equipment market (Ojala, Eloranta, and Jalava 2006). Finland dismantled the state monopoly in telecommunication, first by liberalizing telefax transmission in 1988. The cellular phone business was open to competition from the beginning, which enabled Nokia to develop its capabilities and to supply telecommunication equipment to overseas vendors at competitive prices (Häikiö 2002).

[2]Twenty years earlier, in the 1950s, Ivan Fallon (2007) remembers growing up in a country with "barefoot children, an all-powerful Catholic Church, endless poverty, and mass emigration." He also recalls, "Poetry, song, and a respect and knowledge of age-old culture and mythology."

[3]In the early 1960s, Irish industry comprised mainly producers of food, drinks, tobacco, textiles, and footwear. Half of food exports were live cattle.

[4]The Encouragement of External Investment Act of 1959 repealed restrictions on foreign ownership of industry (White 1983). Ireland was one of the first countries in Europe to actively seek FDI (Ruane and Görg 1999).

[5]FDI policy in Ireland focused on greenfield investment and new industrial segments to minimize competition with domestic firms. In addition, FDI was used to diversify Ireland's economic structure and also the geographic distribution of industry. Many FDI projects were directed to areas outside of Dublin and Cork, the traditional manufacturing bases in Ireland. Part of the aim to attract FDI was to absorb redundant workers from agricultural sectors (Ruane and Görg 1999).

Figure 3.2   Ireland's Industrial Composition, 1970–2007

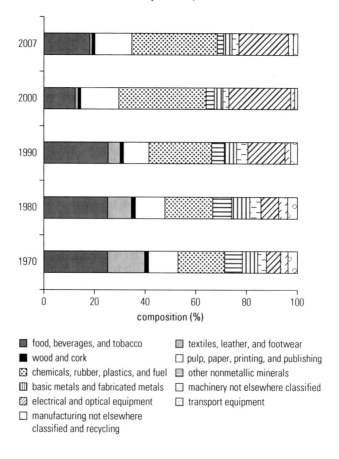

Source: United Nations Industrial Development Organization's INDSTAT3 database.

of food ingredients and flavors); the Linden Food Group (a meat processor); Diageo (which supplies premium drinks, including Guinness); and CRH (a major producer of construction materials) serve as Ireland's standard bearers.

In 1970, the Singaporean economy depended highly on rubber, petrochemical, and food products and produced hardly any electronic products (see figure 3.3). By 2000, the electronics subsector contributed almost half of the industrial output, and the share of chemical products had risen significantly. In contrast, the shares of the petroleum product, rubber, and food sectors had declined. This redrawing of the industrial map was the direct outcome of diversification guided by strategic investments in human capital, infrastructure, and smart urbanization that attracted FDI.

Figure 3.3 Singapore's Industrial Composition, 1970–2007

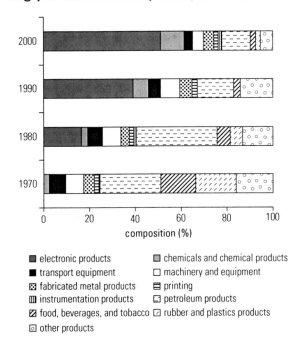

composition (%)

■ electronic products   ▨ chemicals and chemical products
■ transport equipment   □ machinery and equipment
▧ fabricated metal products   ▤ printing
▥ instrumentation products   ▢ petroleum products
▨ food, beverages, and tobacco   ▨ rubber and plastics products
▨ other products

Source: Department of Statistics, various years.

The Rise of High-Tech Exports

The changing composition of domestic industries in the Sifire countries was mir-
rored by the mix of exports. Among Finland's top 10 export commodities in 1970,
nine products were from the wood subsector and the pulp and paper subsector;
ships were the only export commodity that was not resource based (see table 3.1).
By 2000, telecommunication equipment had displaced lumber as the leading
export (see table 3.2). Resource-based products continued to be well represented
among the top 10 export commodities, but their composition also had begun
shifting toward medium- and high-tech products.

Unlike Finland, the export composition of Ireland was radically altered
between 1970 and the end of the century. In 1970, Ireland's main exports were
food products, such as meat and butter, along with clothing and medical
instruments—a mix very different from that of Finland (see table 3.3). With
the exception of medical instruments, all of the other leading exports from the
1970s had been displaced by the end of the century (see table 3.4). Instead, the
list was dominated by high-tech products (electronics and telecommunication

Table 3.1 Finland's Top 10 Exports in 1970, by Value

Rank	Description	Value (US$ million)	Technology class
1	Lumber, sawn, planed, and so forth: conifer	217.1	RB1
2	Sulfate wood pulp	161.0	RB1
3	Newsprint paper	150.3	RB1
4	Ships and boats, other than warships	147.6	MT3
5	Other printing and writing paper, machine made	128.3	RB1
6	Machine-made paper and paperboard, simply finished	114.8	RB1
7	Kraft paper and kraft paperboard	106.0	RB1
8	Plywood, including veneered panels	97.8	RB1
9	Sulfite wood pulp	79.6	RB1
10	Paper and paperboard in rolls or sheets not elsewhere specified	65.4	RB1

Source: United Nations Commodity Trade Statistics Database.
Note: MT3 = engineering products; RB1 = agriculture-based products.

Table 3.2 Finland's Top 10 Exports in 2000, by Value

Rank	Description	Value (US$ million)	Technology class
1	Telecommunication equipment not elsewhere specified	9,685.6	HT1
2	Other printing and writing paper, machine made	3,263.1	RB1
3	Machine-made paper and paperboard, simply finished	2,053.9	RB1
4	Paper and paperboard in rolls or sheets not elsewhere specified	1,599.3	RB1
5	Lumber, sawn, planed, and so forth: conifer	1,459.2	RB1
6	Electric power machinery	1,385.1	Other
7	Ships and boats, other than warships	1,035.2	MT3
8	Sulfate wood pulp	916.5	RB1
9	Passenger motor cars, other than buses	787.9	MT1
10	Motor spirits, gasoline, and other light oils	721.8	RB2

Source: United Nations Commodity Trade Statistics Database.
Note: HT1 = electronics and electrical products; MT1 = automotive products; MT3 = engineering products; RB1 = agriculture-based products; RB2 = resource-based products.

equipment) and pharmaceutical compounds and products (see Honohan and Walsh 2002).

Singapore's principal exports in 1970 were predominantly resource-based products. The country's location and ports enabled Singapore to develop a thriving petrochemicals industry and to earn handsome returns from ship repair—an activity that led to the highly lucrative manufacturing of oil-drilling platforms

Table 3.3 Ireland's Top 10 Exports in 1970, by Value

Rank	Description	Value (US$ million)	Technology class
1	Meat of bovine animals, fresh, chilled, or frozen	118.8	PP
2	Bovine cattle including buffalo	109.6	PP
3	Petroleum, crude and partly refined	52.6	PP
4	Butter	29.4	RB1
5	Chocolate and other food preparations of cocoa	25.7	RB1
6	Clothing of textile fabric, not knitted or crocheted	22.7	LT1
7	Bacon, ham, and other dried, salted, or smoked pig meat	22.1	RB1
8	Ores and concentrates of zinc	22.0	RB2
9	Medical instruments not elsewhere specified	21.6	MT3
10	Beer including ale, stout, and port	20.2	RB1

Source: United Nations Commodity Trade Statistics Database.
Note: LT1 = textiles and fashion products; MT3 = engineering products; PP = primary products; RB1 = agriculture-based products; RB2 = resource-based products.

Table 3.4 Ireland's Top 10 Exports in 2000, by Value

Rank	Description	Value (US$ million)	Technology class
1	Organic and inorganic and heterocyclic compounds	14,206.0	RB2
2	Statistical machines cards or tapes	9,748.1	HT1
3	Office machines not elsewhere specified	8,050.4	HT1
4	Thermionic valves and tubes, transistors, and so forth	4,165.6	HT1
5	Phonograph records, recorded tapes, and other sound recordings	4,020.7	LT2
6	Medicaments	3,725.7	HT2
7	Telecommunication equipment not elsewhere specified	3,174.8	HT1
8	Synthetic perfume and flavor materials and concentrates	1,592.2	RB2
9	Chemical products and preparations not elsewhere specified	1,418.3	MT2
10	Medical instruments, not elsewhere specified	1,243.7	MT3

Source: United Nations Commodity Trade Statistics Database.
Note: HT1 = electronics and electrical products; HT2 = other high-technology products; LT2 = other low-technology products; MT2 = process industries (chemicals and basic metals); MT3 = engineering products; RB2 = resource-based products.

and other structures by Keppel Offshore & Marine[6] (see table 3.5). The export composition of Singapore, like that of Ireland, changed markedly between 1970 and 2000. Although petrochemical products remained in the top 10, other

---

[6]See Keppel's website at http://www.kepcorp.com/en/content.aspx?sid=80 for more information about the company.

resource-based products were replaced by high-tech products—mainly electronics and telecommunication equipment (see table 3.6).

The change in export composition of the three countries is striking evidence of technological catch-up and, in Finland's case, of pushing the frontiers of technology by dint of investment in learning (see figures 3.4–3.6). In 1970, more than half

Table 3.5   Singapore's Top 10 Exports in 1970, by Value

Rank	Description	Value (US$ million)	Technology class
1	Natural rubber and similar natural gums	383.2	PP
2	Motor spirits, gasoline, and other light oils	143.3	RB2
3	Lamp oil and white spirits	66.3	RB2
4	Residual fuel oils	66.0	RB2
5	Distillate fuels	52.7	RB2
6	Lumber, sawn, planed, and so forth: nonconifer	34.2	RB1
7	Pepper and pimento	34.1	PP
8	Coffee, green or roasted	30.0	PP
9	Palm oil	28.3	RB1
10	Lubricating oils and greases	25.3	RB2

Source: United Nations Commodity Trade Statistics Database.
Note: PP = primary products; RB1 = agriculture-based products; RB2 = resource-based products.

Table 3.6   Singapore's Top 10 Exports in 2000, by Value

Rank	Description	Value (US$ million)	Technology class
1	Statistical machine cards or tapes	6,828.2	HT1
2	Distillate fuels	3,788.6	RB2
3	Thermionic valves and tubes, transistors, and so forth	3,674.6	HT1
4	Telecommunication equipment not elsewhere specified	2,027.5	HT1
5	Office machines not elsewhere specified	2,024.5	HT1
6	Lamp oil and white spirits	1,907.9	RB2
7	Motor spirits, gasoline, and other light oils	1,854.6	RB2
8	Radio broadcast receivers	1,575.9	MT3
9	Phonographs, tape and other sound recorders, and so forth	1,419.4	MT3
10	Residual fuel oils	1,335.0	RB2

Source: United Nations Commodity Trade Statistics Database.
Note: HT1 = electronics and electrical products; MT3 = engineering products; RB2 = resource-based products.

Figure 3.4   Finland's Composition of Exports by Technology Class, 1970 and 2000

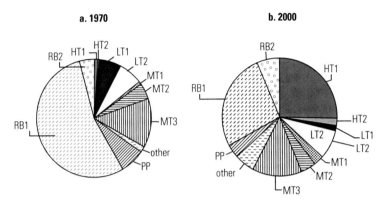

Source: Authors' calculations using data from the United Nations Commodity Trade Statistics Database.
Note: HT1 = electronics and electrical products; HT2 = other high-technology products; LT1 = textiles and fashion products; LT2 = other low-technology products; MT1 = automotive products; MT2 = process industries (chemicals and basic metals); MT3 = engineering products; PP = primary products; RB1 = agriculture-based products; RB2 = resource-based products.

Figure 3.5   Ireland's Composition of Exports by Technology Class, 1970 and 2000

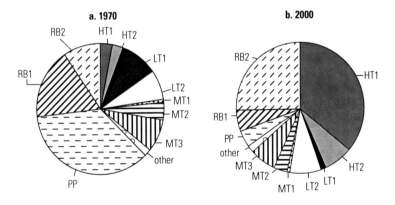

Source: Authors' calculations using data from the United Nations Commodity Trade Statistics Database.
Note: HT1 = electronics and electrical products; HT2 = other high-technology products; LT1 = textiles and fashion products; LT2 = other low-technology products; MT1 = automotive products; MT2 = process industries (chemicals and basic metals); MT3 = engineering products; PP = primary products; RB1 = agriculture-based products; RB2 = resource-based products.

of Finland's and Ireland's exports and close to three-quarters of the exports of Singapore were of resource-based or processed goods. By 2000, they accounted for less than one-third of the exports of Finland and Ireland and less than one-fourth of Singapore's exports. What was so notable by the end of the century was the sheer scale of high-tech exports from these economies, clearly demonstrating the

Figure 3.6   Singapore's Composition of Exports by Technology Class, 1970 and 2000

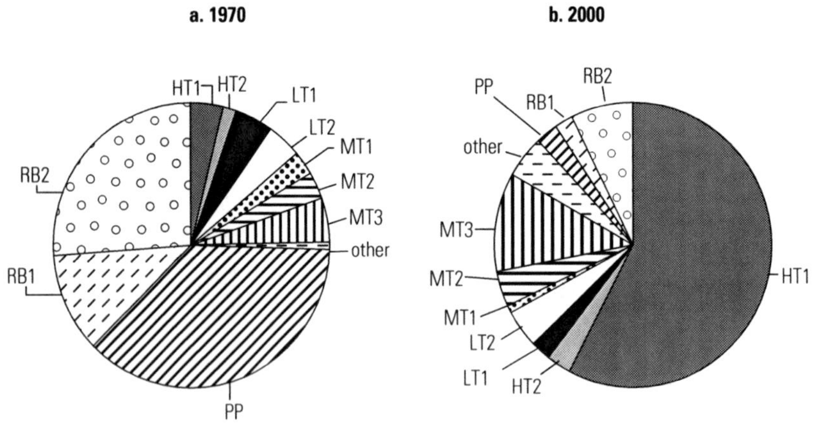

a. 1970

b. 2000

Source: Authors' calculations using data from the United Nations Commodity Trade Statistics Database.
Note: HT1 = electronics and electrical products; HT2 = other high-technology products; LT1 = textiles and fashion products; LT2 = other low-technology products; MT1 = automotive products; MT2 = process industries (chemicals and basic metals); MT3 = engineering products; PP = primary products; RB1 = agriculture-based products; RB2 = resource-based products.

diversification of industry and the huge strides in manufacturing and technological capabilities.[7]

Education Sector: An Overview

The economic transformation from 1970 onward was made possible by the accumulation of human capital in these countries.[8] On average, public spending on education by Sifire was approximately 4 percent of gross domestic product (GDP) between 1980 and 2000. Finland and Ireland were already a little higher as early as the 1970s. Singapore was somewhat lower. Public spending on education by Organisation for Economic Co-operation and Development (OECD) countries

---

[7]Further diversification into the creative industries might be a necessary step for all three economies, and Finland is showing the way with recent successes in the electronic games industry by companies such as Rovio Mobile (the producer of Angry Birds) and Rocket Pack.

[8]In wooing foreign investors, Ireland emphasized the youthfulness of its workforce, and although MNCs attached importance to the low corporate income tax rates Ireland offered, the quality and English-language skills of Irish workers were an important draw. The increase in Ireland's working-age population is related to the legalization of contraception in 1980, which led to a sharp decline in fertility. This youth dividend contributed to Ireland's performance from 1990 to 2005. However, lower rates of fertility will result in rapid aging in the coming decades (Bloom and Canning 2003).

Table 3.7   Public Expenditure on Education, 1970–2006

Indicator	Share (%)					
	1970	**1980**	**1990**	**1995**	**2000**	**2006**
Finland						
Share of GDP	5.7	5.1	5.4	7.0	6.0	6.1
Share of total government expenditure	—	10.9	11.9	12.2	12.2	12.6
Ireland						
Share of GDP	4.6	5.8	4.7	5.0	4.3	4.8
Share of total government expenditure	10.8	10.9	10.2	13.5	13.5	14.0
Singapore						
Share of GDP	3.2	2.7	3.0	3.1	3.7	3.2[a]
Share of total government expenditure	11.7	8.1	19.5	23.5	—	11.6[a]

Source: World Bank's EdStats database.
Note: — = not available.
a. Data are for 2009.

has averaged about 5 percent of GDP since 1975 (see table 3.7). Finland has consistently remained above this level, and both Ireland and Singapore are below the OECD norm. OECD countries have allocated about 12.5 percent of public spending to education, with Finland almost on par with the OECD average. Ireland has allocated more to education since 1995. The smaller size of the government sector in Singapore and initially lower allocation for education explains why its ratio is the smallest. Budgetary allocation was raised in the 1990s. Once private spending is factored in, overall outlay on education is higher than the global average. The notable factor about education in Finland is that it is entirely free at all levels, while this is not the case in the other two countries. Table 3.8 shows the share of public spending on education allocated to the primary, secondary, and tertiary levels.

As early as 1960, the average years of schooling in Finland and Ireland were already relatively high: nearly six years and just exceeding six years, respectively. Singapore, at slightly more than four years, was well short of the other two (see figure 3.7). From early on, these countries made expansion of education access a policy priority.[9] With rising enrollments at all levels of education, the average

---

[9] Singapore's first Five-Year Plan gave priority to free primary education, with an emphasis on mathematics, science, and technical subjects. Spending was increased after 1965, and the government redoubled its efforts to recruit teachers and instituted a free textbooks program (Goh and Gopinathan 2008).

Table 3.8 Share of Public Expenditure for Education, 1970–2007

Education level	Share of total public education expenditure (%)				
	1970	1980	1992	2001	2007
Finland					
Primary	—	—	25.8	21.6	20.4
Secondary	44.4	38.8	38.0	40.1	42.6
Tertiary[a]	8.8	18.0	28.5	32.9	31.4
Ireland					
Primary	—	22.6	27.2	31.9	35.1
Secondary	34.3	34.0	37.6	34.4	34.3
Tertiary[a]	11.7	15.3	19.9	28.6	23.4
Singapore					
Primary	—	—	—	28.1	21.6
Secondary	31.5	35.2	27.1	29.1	24.8
Tertiary[a]	13.8	14.6	24.6	26.9	34.4

Source: World Bank's EdStats database.
Note: — = not available.

Figure 3.7 Average Years of Schooling for People 15-Years-Old and Above, 1960–2000

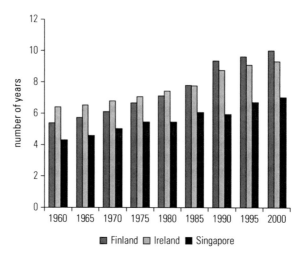

Source: Barro and Lee 2000.

Figure 3.8   Public Expenditure per Student

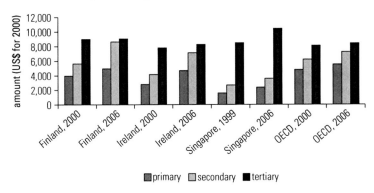

■ primary   ☐ secondary   ■ tertiary

Source: World Bank's World Development Indicators database.

years of schooling in the Sifire countries increased. Finland passed Ireland in 1985, and by 2000, it was the leader, with years of average schooling equaling 10 years compared to 7 in Singapore.

In 2000, Finland was spending about US$4,000 on primary school students, US$5,600 on secondary school students, and US$9,000 on students enrolled in a tertiary-level institution. Singapore's outlay in 2000 was US$1,600 on primary, US$2,700 on secondary, and US$8,500 on tertiary education. By the turn of the century, these countries were assigning greater importance to tertiary education than were the OECD countries as a group (see figure 3.8). In 2006, all three considerably increased the spending per student in secondary education to almost 40 percent of total education expenditure. Per student expenditure for primary education increased, but by a smaller amount. Spending on tertiary education rose further between 2000 and 2006, with Singapore showing the largest increase.

Primary Education

Preschool and primary education—in terms of quantity and quality—are the foundation for later academic prowess and scientific literacy.[10] High enrollment in primary education is desirable to support an expansion of secondary and tertiary education in line with development needs, and the quality of primary education has a profound bearing on later academic achievement. Ireland and Singapore achieved close to universal primary education by 1970,[11] and Finland did so by

---

[10] The contribution of schooling to nation building motivated investment in Finland in the early decades of the 20th century.

[11] Mass primary education was the first objective of the Singapore government during the "survival-driven" phase of development—1959 to 1978 (Shanmugaratnam 2009).

Table 3.9   Primary Enrollment, 1970–2007

Indicator	Share of eligible population (%)						
	1970	1980	1990	1995	1999	2002	2007
Finland							
Gross enrollment	82	98	99	99	99	102	98
Net enrollment	—	—	98	99	99	100	96
Ireland							
Gross enrollment	107	101	103	102	104	104	105
Net enrollment	93	90	90	91	93	95	97
Singapore							
Gross enrollment	105	108	104	95	—	—	—
Net enrollment	94	99	96	93	—	—	—

Source: World Bank's World Development Indicators database.
Note: — = not available.

1980 (see table 3.9). As is apparent from the test scores presented later in this chapter, Sifire countries have achieved outstanding results.

Secondary Education

Net enrollment in secondary education rose smartly in Finland and Ireland, from 71 percent and 63 percent, respectively, in 1970 to 93 percent and 80 percent, respectively, in 1990. Singapore brought up the rear with a rate of 44 percent, which was the average for middle-income countries at that time. Gross enrollment rates in all three countries were far higher because of the presence of older students (see table 3.10).

A large fraction of secondary-level students in Finland have pursued vocational training—30 percent and more (see table 3.11).[12] In comparison, vocational and technical enrollments were lower in Ireland and Singapore but were by no means trivial. Arguably, the building of industrial skills through attention to vocational and technical training assisted the growth of Sifire in the 1980s and 1990s.

Singapore, in particular, benefited from this growth. Singapore has offered vocational training as a viable option for students who are not academically inclined and made determined efforts to erase the status gap between general and

---

[12]An even larger percentage of students in Switzerland rely on vocational and technical training as the stepping-stone to a rewarding career. A full two-thirds select from 230 course offerings, either by enrolling part time and combining classroom instruction with apprenticeships at participating host companies or by enrolling full time in a vocational education and training program at a trade or commercial school. The success of Swiss industry is closely linked to the quality and supply of technical skills produced by the various training institutions.

Table 3.10   Secondary Enrollment, 1970–2007

Indicator	Share of eligible population (%)						
	1970	1980	1990	1995	1999	2002	2007
Finland							
Gross enrollment	102	98	114	116	121	126	111
Net enrollment	71	—	93	93	95	94	97
Ireland							
Gross enrollment	74	89	99	113	107	108	113
Net enrollment	63	78	80	86	84	85	88
Singapore							
Gross enrollment	46	60	68	73	—	—	63.2
Net enrollment	44	—	—	—	—	—	—

Source: Singapore data are from World Bank's EdStat and KAM databases; other data are from World Bank's World Development Indicators database.
Note: — = not available.

Table 3.11   Vocational and Technical Enrollment, 2003–2007

Country	Share of total secondary enrollment (%)		
	2003	2005	2007
Finland	35.8	28.6	29.1
Ireland	—	15.9	16.2
Singapore	—	—	12.0

Source: World Bank's EdStats database.
Note: — = not available.

vocational education.[13] Through planning and effective use of employer feedback, Singapore has attempted to match the skills offered by vocational schools with the needs of the private sector. In the initial stage, Singapore collaborated with various major foreign investors on the training of technicians for their factories. The authorities persuaded these investors to train twice the number they required and gave them the first pick of the graduates. The surplus was used as a resource to attract new investors. This strategy relieved constraints on the growth of targeted industrial clusters. It worked until the number of training centers sponsored by the various investors (and their governments) grew to where consolidation became desirable. Thus was born the Nanyang Polytechnic, which became part of

---

[13]Singapore started with the Technical Education Department in the Ministry of Education, created in 1968. In 1979, the Vocational and Technical Training Board was established. A third step was the setting up of the Institute of Technical Education in 1992. For more information about the institute, see its website at http://www.ite.edu.sg/.

the polytechnic system—the Institute of Technical Education (ITE)—in Singapore under the Ministry of Education.[14] The approach to determining the numbers to be trained thereafter involved all the other polytechnics that were engaged with employers (through formal governance arrangements at the institutional level) and factored in projections of labor demand as well as the demands of students. Once the innovation phase of technical training was over, Singapore's institutions focused on mainstreaming and operating a system that was created as a matter of routine to anticipate and meet the evolving demand for skills steadily and efficiently. A rate of employment for graduates approaching 90 percent testifies to the success of the ITE.

Although Finland began attempting to develop its vocational training system as early as the 1970s, serious reform efforts began gaining momentum only in 1991 with the passage of legislation to set up 22 polytechnics. This legislation was formalized in 1995. The Ministry of Education operates 25 regional, multidisciplinary, and relatively autonomous polytechnics that cater to the needs of local industry and help promote regional development.[15]

A number of institutions in Ireland provide vocational training. There are vocational education committee schools, community schools, and local and Department of Employment training centers. Graduates are also eligible for apprenticeship programs. The system benefits from being embedded in a national qualifications framework and from the close collaboration of employers (through the ICT Ireland Skillnet) with social partners and concerned government departments. However, the quality of instructors and students is low; feedback and evaluation are less rigorous than in Singapore, for example, and the overall governance is weaker (see Kis 2010).

Quality of Primary and Secondary Education

Although the data on quality of education across countries are sparse, two international tests can be used to compare student quality. Unfortunately, until recently, Singapore participated only in the Trends in International Mathematics and Science Study (TIMSS),[16] while Finland and Ireland participated in the

---

[14]Training courses are provided in five areas: engineering, business, ICT, applied sciences, and health sciences.

[15]See OECD (2003) for details on the Finnish polytechnic system. A list of the polytechnics can be found on the ministry's website at http://www.minedu.fi/OPM/Koulutus/ ammattikorkeakoulutus/ammattikorkeakoulut/?lang=en.

[16]TIMSS is an international assessment of the mathematics and science knowledge of fourth- and eighth-grade students around the world. TIMSS was developed by the International Association for the Evaluation of Educational Achievement to allow participating nations to compare students' educational achievement across borders. TIMSS data have been collected in 1995, 1999, 2003, and 2007.

Table 3.12   Singapore's TIMSS Ranks and Scores, 1995–2007

Test	2007		2003		1999		1995	
	Rank	Score	Rank	Score	Rank	Score	Rank	Score
Science								
Fourth grade	1	587	1	565	n.a.	n.a.	7	547
Eighth grade	1	567	1	578	2	568	1	607
Math								
Fourth grade	2	599	1	594	n.a.	n.a.	1	625
Eighth grade	3	593	1	605	1	604	1	643

Sources: Mullis, Martin, and Foy (2008); Martin, Mullis, and Foy (2008).
Note: n.a. = not applicable. Fourth grade assessment was not done in 1999.

OECD Programme for International Student Assessment (PISA).[17] Nevertheless, the available information does convey a sense of the quality of education in Sifire relative to comparators. Singapore participated in PISA in 2009 for the first time.

In science, in 2007, students from Singapore led the pack in tests aimed at fourth and eighth graders (see table 3.12). They were also ranked first in the 2003 test. In math, Singaporean students ranked second and third for fourth and eighth graders, respectively, in 2007. Since 1995, Singapore has excelled in math and science for fourth and eighth graders.

Whereas TIMSS has two subject areas, PISA contains three: math, science, and reading.[18] Finland has consistently ranked at or near the top in all categories in the last four rounds of PISA (see table 3.13 for the ranking and test scores in 2009). Compared with Finnish students, Irish students do not fare well, except in science. Their scores for science are above the OECD average. However, their scores for reading are close to the average for OECD countries, and their scores for math are below the OECD average. Singapore, for the first time, participated in the 2009 PISA.[19] Singaporean students, much like their counterparts from Finland, performed outstandingly in all three subjects.

Tertiary Education

Tertiary-level enrollments in Finland and Ireland were near the European average in the 1970s, with Singapore at about half that level (see table 3.14). Finland

---

[17] The OECD's PISA surveys 15-year-olds in the principal industrial countries. Every three years, it assesses how far students near the end of compulsory education have acquired some of the knowledge and skills essential for full participation in society (science, reading, and math). OECD originally created PISA for its own needs, but the assessment is now used as a major policy tool for countries around the world.

[18] PISA is administered by OECD and is aimed mainly at assessing student achievements in OECD countries, but it is open to nonmembers. The first assessment was done in 2000.

[19] Shanghai also participated in PISA 2009, and students from Shanghai placed first for all three subjects.

Table 3.13 PISA Ranks and Scores, 2000–09

Test	Finland Rank	Finland Score	Ireland Rank	Ireland Score	Singapore Rank	Singapore Score
2009						
Science	2	554	20	508	4	542
Reading	3	536	21	496	5	526
Math	6	541	32	487	2	562
2006						
Science	1	563	20	508	n.a.	n.a.
Reading	2	547	6	517	n.a.	n.a.
Math	2	548	22	501	n.a.	n.a.
2003						
Science	1	548	16	505	n.a.	n.a.
Reading	1	543	7	515	n.a.	n.a.
Math	1	544	20	502	n.a.	n.a.
2000						
Science	3	538	9	513	n.a.	n.a.
Reading	1	546	5	526	n.a.	n.a.
Math	4	536	15	502	n.a.	n.a.

Source: OECD 2009.
Note: n.a. = not applicable.

was the first of the three to expand its tertiary education sector at a rapid pace. Between 1970 and 1980, the enrollment rates more than doubled, and since then they have continued to increase, reaching 94 percent in 2007, one of the highest in the world. The expansion of the tertiary education sector in Ireland came a decade later. A serious push started in the 1980s, but the most rapid increase occurred in the early 1990s. By 2000, the gross enrollment rate in Ireland was almost 50 percent. Singapore also began expanding tertiary enrollment in the early 1990s. With almost 50 percent of secondary school graduates going on to earn university degrees, the gross enrollment rate more than doubled over the course of the decade (see table 3.14).[20]

Between 1980 and 2001, the proportion of the workforce with tertiary-level qualifications rose in all three countries. The increase was greatest in Finland and least in Ireland (see table 3.15). Equally important for the purposes of increasing technological and manufacturing capabilities was the high percentage of students who majored in science, engineering, and math, a testimony to the quality of

---

[20]One-fourth of the Singapore government's expenditures are on education and, of this amount, 40 percent is for tertiary education (Shanmugaratnam 2009).

Table 3.14 Tertiary-Level Education Gross Enrollment Rates, 1970–2007

Country	Gross enrollment rate (%)						
	1970	1980	1990	1997	2000	2005	2007
Finland	13	32	45	74	83	92	94
Ireland	12	17	28	43	49	58	61
Singapore	6	8	18	44	—	—	56

Source: Singapore data are from World Bank's EdStat and KAM databases; Finland and Ireland data are from the World Bank's World Development Indicators database.
Note: — = not available.

Table 3.15 Labor Force with Tertiary Education, 1995–2006

Country	Share of total labor force (%)		
	1995	2001	2006
Finland	20.7	31.6	33.7
Ireland	24.3	25.8	42.1
Singapore	33.2	37.9	—

Source: World Bank's World Development Indicators database.
Note: — = not available.

instruction and the scientific literacy imparted in primary and secondary schools.[21]

Close to one-half of tertiary-level students in Singapore were enrolled in science and engineering fields in 2007. In Finland, science and engineering fields have attracted about one-third of the student body, whereas in Ireland, about one-fifth of students are enrolled in science and engineering fields (see table 3.16).

Data on degrees awarded provides additional insight into the accumulation of scientific capital. Close to 20 percent of degrees awarded to university graduates in Finland in the early 1980s were in the fields of science and technology. Later in the decade, there was a steep decline, with only a handful of graduates earning degrees

---

[21] From the 1970s, the number of students studying science, technology, and IT-related subjects in Ireland steadily increased, and by the 1990s, the ratio of such students to the total number enrolled in tertiary education was the highest in the EU. This increase catered to demand generated by MNCs and was not in support of domestic research and development, which remained low. Almost 40 percent of tertiary-level students took two-year nonuniversity courses in science and technology subjects, which helped quickly boost the supply of skilled workers at low cost. However, even in the mid 1990s, half of the labor force was not competent to participate in the knowledge economy because the IT skills of teachers and students were low (Crafts 2005; O'Toole 2009).

Table 3.16   Tertiary-Level Enrollment Composition, 2007

Field	Finland		Ireland		Singapore	
	Students enrolled	Ratio (%)	Students enrolled	Ratio (%)	Students enrolled	Ratio (%)
Education	15,961	5.2	10,610	5.6	5,794	3.1
Humanities and arts	45,171	14.6	27,984	14.7	16,531	8.9
Social sciences, business, and law	70,275	22.7	41,964	22.0	65,542	35.1
Science and engineering	113,299	36.6	40,553	21.3	87,306	46.8
Agriculture	6,893	2.2	2,367	1.2	0	0.0
Health and welfare	42,376	13.7	24,852	13.1	10,307	5.5
Services	15,188	4.9	9,261	4.9	1,147	0.6
Nonspecified programs	n.a.	n.a.	32,758	17.2	n.a.	n.a.

Source: United Nations Educational, Scientific, and Cultural Organization Institute for Statistics.
Note: n.a. = not applicable.

in science and engineering (figure 3.9). This downturn was quickly reversed, and by the mid 1990s, 28 percent of students in Finland were receiving degrees in science and engineering fields compared with 35 percent in Ireland and 54 percent in Singapore in 2000 (table 3.17). Since then, the share of graduates in science and engineering fields has been largely maintained in Finland and Singapore, although in Ireland, the share had dropped to 24 percent by 2007, and the trend in enrollments points to a further decline in the future (table 3.18).

To maintain their competitive edge, both Finland and Singapore are emphasizing cross-disciplinary education, which straddles science, engineering, design, and business studies and equips students with technical and entrepreneurial skills.[22] Singapore has created a new university to meet this objective, and Finland merged the Helsinki University of Technology, the School of Economics, and the University of Art and Design to create a highly selective, legally private, and potentially world-class Aalto University.[23] A point that bears noting is that both Ireland and Singapore have demonstrated a readiness to adopt flexible immigration and visa issuance policies. Such policies allow them to tap the international market for skills, thus overcoming domestic shortages and skill mismatches, and, in Singapore's case, to accommodate the pursuit of diversification into high-tech

---

[22]Encouraging risk taking and entrepreneurship is a key objective; in Finland, as in many East Asian economies, failure in business has long been viewed as an inerasable stigma.

[23]Finland has discovered that a small country cannot afford 20 universities and 25 polytechnics and is currently engaged in a process of rationalization through merger. See Aarrevaara, Dobson, and Elander (2009).

Figure 3.9   Composition of Graduates in Finland, Tertiary Education, 1981–99

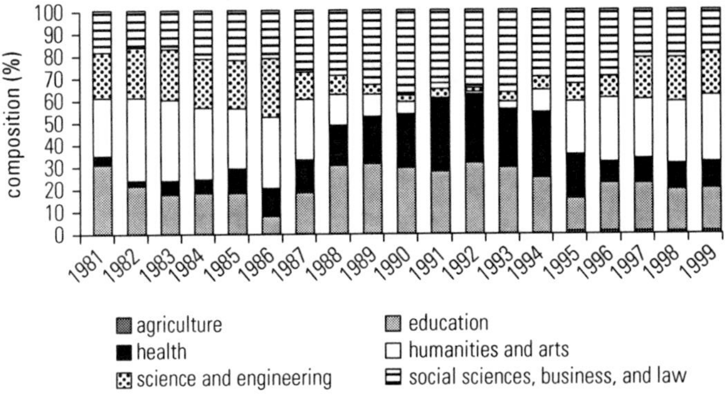

Source: Finnish Ministry of Education's KOTA database (https://kotaplus.csc.fi/online/Haku.do).

Table 3.17   Composition of Tertiary Education Graduates, 2000

	Share of total graduates (%)						
Country	Education	Humanities and arts	Social sciences, business, and law	Science and engineering	Agriculture	Health	Services
Finland	7	12	23	28	3	22	6
Ireland	6	16	31	35	1	8	3
Singapore	1	8	25	54	0	8	1

Source: For Finland and Ireland, United Nations Educational, Scientific, and Cultural Organization Institute for Statistics; for Singapore, Ministry of Education.
Note: Data for Singapore are for 1999. For Singapore, humanities and arts include social sciences.

activities. In 2006, foreigners comprised close to a third of Singapore's labor force—90,000 of whom were skilled workers (Yeoh 2007). Similarly, in 2006, foreigners accounted for an eighth of Ireland's labor force—almost a quarter of a million workers—when a decade earlier there had been hardly any.[24] In adopting this approach, Ireland and Singapore have followed the example of Switzerland, a country that has long relied on foreign sources to close frictional skill and knowledge gaps and sustain industrial momentum. As a consequence, more than a fifth of Switzerland's population is foreign born.[25]

---

[24]Some 345,000 workers from the 10 countries that joined the EU on May 1, 2004, were registered to work in Ireland in 2006 (*Migration News* 2006).

[25]Switzerland's student pool has a high share of foreigners, and well more than a third of doctoral degrees from Swiss institutions are awarded to foreign students. Swiss firms recruit from this pool; hence, immigration and labor market regulations, including work permits, are key issues (OECD 2006, 39, 81).

Table 3.18   Composition of Tertiary Education Graduates, 2007

	Share of total graduates (%)						
Country	Education	Humanities and arts	Social sciences, business, and law	Science and engineering	Agriculture	Health	Services
Finland	7	15	23	29	2	19	6
Ireland	7	25	28	24	1	12	2
Singapore	4	11	22	51	0	7	1

Source: For Finland and Ireland, United Nations Educational, Scientific, and Cultural Organization Institute for Statistics; for Singapore, Ministry of Education.
Note: For Singapore, humanities and arts include social sciences.

Research Output

Adequate, good-quality science, technology, engineering, and mathematics skills are a necessary precondition for technological catch-up and innovation. Another precondition is a research culture that stimulates technology absorption, knowledge deepening, and innovation. In addition to the direct benefits, research creates jobs, produces the human capital needed to put new ideas into practice, and brings into existence a physical and social infrastructure supportive of innovation. The research output of universities and research institutes points to the scale and sophistication of the scientific establishment and to its capacity to both absorb ideas from abroad and push the frontiers of science and technology.

Universities are at the core of the scientific establishment, and their research caliber can be gauged from a number of indicators. One is through tallying the number of papers published in scientific and technical journals. In 1981, researchers in Finland published 2,173 scientific and technical journal articles (table 3.19). This output is respectable but not outstanding. (For instance, the number published by German residents was 26,837.) Researchers in Ireland published 700 papers in 1981, and those in Singapore published 124. In all three countries, the pace of publication picked up in the 1990s. Singapore's output doubled every five years starting in 1981, although it started from a low base. Nonetheless, by 1995, the scientific output of Singapore matched that of Ireland, and by 2000, it surpassed Ireland and was a little under half of Finland's output. This trend reflects Singapore's effort to expand the tertiary sector and to improve the quality of both teaching and research.

Citations to papers are an index of quality. By field of specialization, Finland has the greatest influence on agricultural sciences, physics, and clinical medicine (see table 3.20). For instance, papers in the agriculture sciences by Finnish researchers received 57 percent more citations than the world average in that field. As a share of total world publications, the top fields for Finland are environment

Table 3.19   Scientific and Technical Journal Articles, 1981–2005

Country	Number of articles					
	1981	1985	1990	1995	2000	2005
Finland	2,173	2,485	3,071	4,077	4,844	4,811
Ireland	700	653	902	1,218	1,581	2,120
Singapore	124	289	572	1,141	2,361	3,609

Source: World Bank's World Development Indicators database.

Table 3.20   Impact of Finnish Papers, 2004–08

Field	Share of world publications (%)	Impact (%)
Agricultural sciences	0.95	57
Physics	0.80	57
Clinical medicine	1.04	43
Environment and ecology	1.77	34
Geosciences	1.00	32
Plant and animal sciences	1.03	26
Engineering	0.77	20
Mathematics	0.66	13
Pharmacology and toxicology	0.82	10
Psychiatry and psychology	0.96	6

Source: Thomson Reuters's Science Watch (http://sciencewatch.com/dr/sci/09/oct18-09_2/).
Note: The data are based on 43,795 papers that listed at least one author's address in Finland between 2004 and 2008. The impact is calculated as the relative number of Finnish citations to the world average in each field.

and ecology, space science, and computer sciences. The latter two are not listed in the table because of their low-impact value.

Ireland has many high-impact papers in material sciences, immunology, and physics (see table 3.21). By share, papers in the agriculture sciences are ranked highest, followed by those in space science and microbiology. Part of the reason for Ireland's strong performance in agriculture sciences is the traditional focus on this sector and the establishment in 2003 of the Science Foundation Ireland, which aims to raise Ireland's profile in the biosciences and ICT. Part of the foundation's responsibility is to recruit promising scientists and engineers from overseas (Rios-Morales and Brennan 2009).

Thomson Reuters's Science Watch, the source for the data in tables 3.20 and 3.21, did not analyze the impact of papers from Singapore; however, engineering is one of the strengths of tertiary institutions in the city-state. Nanyang Technological University ranked eighth, and National University of Singapore

Table 3.21 Impact of Irish Scientific Papers, 2004–08

Field	Share of world publications (%)	Impact (%)
Materials science	0.36	59
Immunology	0.52	49
Physics	0.45	44
Agricultural sciences	1.12	30
Chemistry	0.29	26
Space science	0.78	19
Geosciences	0.40	18
Engineering	0.43	14
Microbiology	0.71	11
Neuroscience and behavior	0.42	11

Source: Thomson Reuters's Science Watch (http://sciencewatch.com/dr/sci/10/feb7-10_2/).
Note: The data are based on 22,789 papers that listed at least one author's address in Ireland between 2004 and 2008. The impact is calculated as the relative number of Irish citations to the world average in each field.

ninth, in the top 20 engineering institutions in the world, on the basis of citations received by papers published between 1999 and 2009.[26]

Ranking of Universities

The university scorecard, which is based on a number of criteria, provides another window on technological and innovation capacity. By these criteria, the three countries are well positioned, although not anywhere near the forefront. Among Sifire institutions, the National University of Singapore occupied 30th place in 2009, followed by Trinity College Dublin at 43rd, Nanyang Technological University at 73rd, and University College Dublin at 89th (see table 3.22). The highest-ranking university in Finland was the University of Helsinki, at 108th.

Innovation Capabilities

Sifire invested very little in research and development (R&D) during the 1970s and early 1980s, and innovation capability was modest. At that time, the main economic activities in the three countries were not R&D intensive. Finland's

---

[26]The highest-ranking Asian institution (seventh place) was the Chinese Academy of Science. The University of Tokyo ranked 17th, and the Indian Institutes of Technology ranked 11th. See http://sciencewatch.com/inter/ins/10/10febTOP20ENG/.

Table 3.22   Ranking of Universities, 2009

University	Country	Rank
National University of Singapore	Singapore	30
Trinity College Dublin	Ireland	43
Nanyang Technological University	Singapore	73
University College Dublin	Ireland	89

Source: QS World University Rankings (http://www.topuniversities.com/).

Table 3.23   R&D Expenditure, 1996–2007

Country	Share of GDP (%)				
	1996	2000	2003	2006	2007
Finland	2.5	3.3	3.4	3.4	3.4
Ireland	1.3	1.1	1.2	1.3	—
Singapore	1.4	1.9	2.1	2.4	—

Source: World Bank's World Development Indicators database.
Note: — = not available.

economy was still heavily dependent on relatively low-tech resource sectors,[27] Ireland's on agriculture and food, and Singapore's on light manufactures.

R&D Spending

Once Sifire embraced a human capital– and technology-led strategy, the tempo of research rose, and Finland and Singapore increased their R&D spending from the mid 1990s (see table 3.23).[28] By 2007, Finland was spending 3.4 percent of GDP on R&D, comparable to high R&D spenders such as Japan and the Republic of Korea. The process leading to this research focus began in the 1980s, when Finland established the Finnish Funding Agency for Technology and Innovation (Tekes) to distribute funding for R&D. In 1987, Tekes functions were augmented by the creation of the Science and Technology Policy Council. Thereafter, the share of innovation supported by public funding rose from less than 20 percent to more than

---

[27]It is not the case that there were no research activities in these areas. The first commercial R&D lab in Finland was established by Alko Oy (the national alcohol company) in 1908. In the 1930s and 1940s, forest industry firms established several joint research labs to share costs of research in such areas as export facilitation, weathering, strength, quality, and so forth (Saarinen 2005).
[28]A rapid increase in R&D in Finland was adopted as a policy goal starting in the 1990s, with the aim of reaching 2.9 percent of GDP by 1999 (Ojala, Eloranta, and Jalava 2006).

Table 3.24   Researchers in R&D, 1984–2006

Country	Number of researchers per million people					
	1984	1987	1996	2000	2003	2006
Finland	—	—	—	6,733	7,998	7,681
Ireland	—	—	1,764	2,239	2,513	2,882
Singapore	879	1,211	2,538	4,140	4,744	5,713

Source: World Bank's World Development Indicators database.
Note: — = not available.

80 percent of GDP (Saarinen 2005). Singapore also increased its spending on R&D in the 1990s, and by 2006, outlay on R&D reached 2.4 percent of GDP. In contrast, Ireland's R&D expenditure has remained around 1 percent of GDP for the past 15 years.

Researchers

As R&D spending rose, so also did the number of researchers in Finland and Singapore (see table 3.24). In 1984, there were fewer than 1,000 researchers per million people in Singapore. By 2006, the number had ballooned to more than 5,700. Finland followed suit with the number of researchers rising from 5 for every 1,000 workers in 1991 to 22 for every 1,000 workers, or almost three times the OECD average (OECD 2010). Even though R&D spending as a share of GDP did not increase in Ireland, the number of researchers climbed from 1,764 in 1996 to 2,882 in 2006, in step with the growing volume of resources devoted to research.

Patents

Scientific publications are one indicator of research output; patents are a second and more sensitive indicator of the commercial potential of research (see table 3.25). In 1970, the U.S. Patent and Trademark Office (USPTO) granted 46 patents to Finnish residents, 12 to Irish residents, and none to Singaporean residents.[29] Compared to the 4,439 patents granted to German residents at that time, the numbers granted to Sifire were small. Much has changed, beginning in the late 1990s. With respect to total patents granted from 1963 to 2009, Finland ranks 16th, Singapore 23rd, and Ireland 28th. Finnish residents garnered the largest number of patents from the mid 1980s onward (see table 3.25), with Singapore and, to a lesser extent, Ireland picking up speed after 1995. But even though the

---

[29]The numbers of patents granted by national patent offices are not comparable because of differences in grant decisions. For international comparison, it is better to use a patent office as a base. Here, data from USPTO are used. USPTO assigns "nationality" of a patent on the basis of the resident country of a first-named inventor of the patent.

Table 3.25   U.S. Patents Granted by Country of Origin, 1970–2008

Country	Number of patents granted								
	1970	1975	1980	1985	1990	1995	2000	2005	2008
Finland	46	98	121	200	304	358	618	720	824
Ireland	12	15	16	30	49	47	121	156	164
Singapore	0	1	3	9	12	53	218	346	399
OECD average	527	768	739	983	1,300	1,238	1,897	1,771	2,014

Source: Data from USPTO.
Note: OECD average excludes the United States.

Table 3.26   Top 10 Technology Classes by the Number of Patents Granted to Residents of Finland in the 1980s

Class number	Class title	Number of patents
162	Paper making and fiber liberation	128
210	Liquid purification or separation	52
73	Measuring and testing	42
29	Metalworking	35
250	Radiant energy	35
34	Drying and gas or vapor contact with solids	32
414	Material or article handling	31
144	Woodworking	31
241	Solid material comminuting or disintegration	30
423	Chemistry of inorganic compounds	27

Source: Data from USPTO.

number of patents granted to Sifire residents during this period rose, compared to the OECD average (excluding the United States),[30] the numbers were still relatively small.

It is not surprising that Finnish residents received most of their patents for technology related to paper making in the 1980s. Not a single patent was for technologies associated with electronics or telecommunication equipment, for which Finland is now famous (see table 3.26). But starting in the 1990s, once Nokia had emerged as an ICT powerhouse, the composition of patenting changed swiftly. Between 2005 and 2009, the technology classes of patents granted to Finnish residents reveal that the bulk of patents are concentrated in

---

[30]The figure for the United States was excluded because for U.S. entities USPTO is a domestic patent office and because U.S.-based organizations tend to apply to USPTO for patents more often than foreign-based entities.

Table 3.27 Top 10 Technology Classes by the Number of Patents Granted to Residents of Finland between 2005 and 2009

Class number	Class title	Number of patents	Share of total patents granted (%)
455	Telecommunications	781	18.6
370	Multiplex communications	494	11.7
375	Pulse or digital communications	190	4.5
162	Paper making and fiber liberation	128	3.0
709	Multicomputer data transferring (electrical computers and digital processing systems)	117	2.8
713	Support (electrical computers and digital processing systems)	72	1.7
128	Surgery (includes class 600)	70	1.7
424	Drug, bioaffecting, and body-treating compositions (includes class 514)	66	1.6
379	Telephonic communications	64	1.5
187	Elevator, industrial lift truck, or stationary lift for vehicle	61	1.4

Source: Data from USPTO.

telecommunication and related technologies, consistent with the changing comparative advantage. Four classes out of 10 listed in table 3.27 are in telecommunications, and 2 are in data transfer. Only 3 percent of all patents are in paper and pulp, although this sector remains one of Finland's key industries and several of the country's largest firms are producers of forest-based products, firms such as Stora Enso, UPM, and Metsäliitto.

Ireland had begun showing some capabilities in electronics and communication technologies by the late 1980s along with technologies associated with the medical industry (drugs and surgery), as was evidenced by the patent statistics (see table 3.28). The trend became more firmly entrenched in the 1990s, and it is highly visible in the data for 2005 to 2009 (see table 3.29). Patents obtained by Irish residents are concentrated in computers, semiconductors, and telecommunications, with continuing strength in medical fields, especially surgical instruments.

During the 1980s, Singapore received few patents from the USPTO, and most were related to machinery (see table 3.30). It is difficult to imagine from these earlier data that Singapore would emerge as an important innovator in electronics and the semiconductor industry, which is what transpired in less than two decades. By 2009, Singapore was clearly specialized in semiconductor and computer-related technologies (see table 3.31). In fact, all the top 10 classes belong to a broad definition of electronics, IT, and telecommunication devices.

Table 3.28 Top 10 Technology Classes by the Number of Patents Granted to Residents of Ireland in the 1980s

Class number	Class title	Number of patents
156	Adhesive bonding and miscellaneous chemical manufacture	12
340	Communications: electrical	10
424	Drug, bioaffecting, and body-treating compositions	9
318	Electricity: motive power systems	9
360	Dynamic magnetic information storage or retrieval	8
128	Surgery	8
525	Synthetic resins or natural rubbers (part of the class 520 series)	7
250	Radiant energy	7
526	Synthetic resins or natural rubbers (part of the class 520 series)	6
200	Electricity: circuit makers and breakers	5

Source: Data from USPTO.

Table 3.29 Top 10 Technology Classes by the Number of Patents Granted to Residents of Ireland between 2005 and 2009

Class number	Class title	Number of patents	Share of total patents granted (%)
341	Coded data generation or conversion	36	4.4
424	Drug, bioaffecting, and body-treating compositions (includes class 514)	33	4.0
370	Multiplex communications	29	3.5
606	Surgery (instruments)	24	2.9
709	Multicomputer data transferring (electrical computers and digital processing systems)	23	2.8
327	Miscellaneous active electrical nonlinear devices, circuits, and systems	20	2.4
375	Pulse or digital communications	20	2.4
128	Surgery (includes class 600)	19	2.3
455	Telecommunications	18	2.2
257	Active solid-state devices (for example, transistors, solid-state diodes)	17	2.1

Source: Data from USPTO.

Table 3.30   Top 10 Technology Classes by the Number of Patents Granted to Residents of Singapore in the 1980s

Class number	Class title	Number of patents
89	Ordnance	7
166	Wells	5
29	Metalworking	3
273	Amusement devices: games	3
118	Coating apparatus	2
405	Hydraulic and earth engineering	2
47	Plant husbandry	2
206	Special receptacle or package	2
361	Electricity: electrical systems and devices	2
351	Optics: eye examining, vision testing, and correcting	2
56	Harvesters	2
173	Tool driving or impacting	2

Source: Data from USPTO.

Table 3.31   Top 10 Technology Classes by the Number of Patents Granted to Residents of Singapore between 2005 and 2009

Class number	Class title	Number of patents	Share of total patents granted (%)
438	Semiconductor device manufacturing: process	307	15.5
257	Active solid-state devices (for example, transistors, solid-state diodes)	237	11.9
360	Dynamic magnetic information storage or retrieval	99	5.0
385	Optical waveguides	42	2.1
330	Amplifiers	41	2.1
375	Pulse or digital communications	39	2.0
324	Electricity: measuring and testing	38	1.9
439	Electrical connectors	35	1.8
455	Telecommunications	32	1.6
327	Miscellaneous active electrical nonlinear devices, circuits, and systems	29	1.5

Source: Data from USPTO.

Table 3.32   Top 10 Assignees by the Number of Patents Granted to Residents of Finland in the 1980s

First-named assignee	Number of patents
Individuals	513
Valmet Oy	173
Outokumpu Oy	120
Oy Wärtsilä Ab	94
Oy Tampella Ab	90
A. Ahlström Osakeyhtiö	68
Neste Oy	42
Enso-Gutzeit Oy	39
Elevator GmbH	32
Labsystems Oy	25

Source: Data from USPTO.

A glance at the top 10 entities that actually hold the right to patents assigned to Finnish residents in the 1980s reveals that most patents were granted to individuals, followed by Valmet, a state-owned machinery maker;[31] Outokumpu, then a mining company; Wärtsilä, a diesel engine maker; and Tampella, a heavy industry manufacturer (see table 3.32). Since the beginning of the 21st century, Nokia has dominated innovation in Finland and has received more than half of all patents granted to Finnish assignees between 2005 and 2009 (see table 3.33).[32,33]

Even though there was no concentration on specific technology classes in Ireland, the data on assignees indicate clearly that electronics, IT, telecommunication, and medical firms are the major areas of specialization (see tables 3.34 and 3.35).

---

[31]Valmet merged with Rauma in 1999 to become Metso.

[32]Nokia opened its first R&D unit in 1960 (Saarinen 2005), and it accounts for one-third of R&D expenditures and about half of business R&D (Ojala, Eloranta, and Jalava 2006). Finland's grasping of first-mover advantages through innovation are discussed by Lester (2005).

[33]Nokia sits at the center of Finland's ICT cluster in Oulu and other cities, which consists of almost 6,000 firms. Some 300 of those firms are first-tier subcontractors to Nokia (see OECD 2000). The ICT cluster is by far the most innovative segment of the economy, with firms receiving technical know-how from Nokia. It generates 10 percent of Finland's GDP, with Nokia accounting for 3.5 percent alone (Ylä-Anttila 2007; Ylä-Anttila and Palmberg 2007). However, the cluster is weakly interlinked with the rest of the economy (Daveri and Silva 2004).

Table 3.33 Top 10 Assignees by the Number of Patents Granted to Residents of Finland between 2005 and 2009

First-named assignee	Number of patents	Share of total patents granted (%)
Nokia Corporation	1,964	54.9
Metso Paper Inc.	185	5.2
Nokia Mobile Phones Ltd.	153	4.3
Individuals	124	3.5
KONE Corporation	92	2.6
ABB Oy	77	2.2
Nokia Networks Oy	73	2.0
Telefonaktiebolaget LM Ericsson	44	1.2
ASM International NV	43	1.2
Instrumentarium Corp.	33	0.9

Source: Data from USPTO.

Foreign subsidiaries play a significant role in national R&D in Ireland[34] (Rios-Morales and Brennan 2009); hence, many assignees are MNCs.[35]

Similarly, many assignees in Singapore are well-known foreign manufacturers of electronics and semiconductors. Such companies already topped the list of assignees in the 1980s (see table 3.36), and the dominance of well-known MNCs has become more apparent in recent years (see table 3.37). What is notable is the relatively large share of patents assigned to the Agency for Science, Technology, and Research (A*STAR)[36]—a public research organization—and to the National University of Singapore. Furthermore, none of the assignees are as dominant as in Finland and Ireland, pointing to a broader base of innovation activities in Singapore resulting from R&D by MNCs in several fields. This broader base also reflects on the quality of the research talent and the infrastructure in Singapore.

---

[34]From early on, Ireland relied on foreign subsidiaries for R&D. In 1995, foreign subsidiaries accounted for 65 percent of business R&D expenditure. In 1993, foreign firms accounted for 95 percent of R&D expenditures in the pharmaceutical industry, 78 percent in the software industry, and 64 percent in the automotive industry (Kearns and Ruane 2001).

[35]USPTO classifies the nationality of a patent by the nationality of the first inventor. Therefore, if the first-mentioned inventor is residing in Ireland, the patent is considered Irish even though it may be assigned to a firm located elsewhere.

[36]A*STAR is Singapore's principal research organization and the driving force behind programs for building research capability, such as the Biopolis project.

Table 3.34 Top 10 Assignees by the Number of Patents Granted to Residents of Ireland in the 1980s

First-named assignee	Number of patents
Loctite (Ireland) Limited	38
Kollmorgen Technologies Corporation	10
Institute for Industrial Research and Standards	6
Elan Corporation Plc	7
Analog Devices Inc.	7
Gallaher Limited	4
Institute for Industrial Research and Standards	4
Security Imprinter Corporation	3
National Research Development Corporation	3
SPS Technologies Inc.	3

Source: Data from USPTO.

Table 3.35 Top 10 Assignees by the Number of Patents Granted to Residents of Ireland between 2005 and 2009

First-named assignee	Number of patents	Share of total patents granted (%)
Analog Devices Inc.	104	21.3
Individuals	67	13.7
Boston Scientific Scimed Inc.	25	5.1
Medtronic Vascular Inc.	23	4.7
Nortel Networks Limited	22	4.5
Loctite (R&D) Limited	19	3.9
Donnelly Corporation	16	3.3
Intel Corporation	16	3.3
TDK Corporation	15	3.1
3Com Corporation	14	2.9

Source: Data from USPTO.

Innovation Facilitator

International trade mediates technology flow through the imports, FDI, and direct trading of technologies.[37] Imports, particularly of capital goods, transfer embedded technologies. FDI stimulates exporting activities and builds technological

---

[37]See Nabeshima (2004) for the various channels of technology transfer.

Table 3.36   Top 10 Assignees by the Number of Patents Granted to Residents of Singapore in the 1980s

First-named assignee	Number of patents
General Electric Company	7
Chartered Industries of Singapore Private Ltd.	7
U.S. Philips Corporation	5
Motorola Inc.	4
Sun Industrial Coatings Private Ltd.	4
Eastern Oil Tools Pte. Ltd.	3
Metro Plastic Industry Pte. Ltd.	2
VARTA AG	1
Everbloom Biotechnology Ltd.	1
Polycore Optical Pte. Ltd.	1

Source: Data from USPTO.

Table 3.37   Top 10 Assignees by the Number of Patents Granted to Residents of Singapore between 2005 and 2009

First-named assignee	Number of patents	Share of total patents granted (%)
Chartered Semiconductor Manufacturing Ltd.	184	11.4
Micron Technology Inc.	154	9.5
Agency for Science, Technology, and Research	136	8.4
Seagate Technology LLC	118	7.3
National University of Singapore	78	4.8
Marvell International Ltd.	72	4.4
STATS ChipPAC Ltd.	62	3.8
Individuals	62	3.8
Hewlett-Packard Development Company LP	58	3.6
STMicroelectronics Asia Pacific Pte. Ltd.	54	3.3

Source: Data from USPTO.

capabilities[38] through spillovers, demonstration effects, training of workers, demand for higher-skilled workers, and technical assistance given to upstream and downstream firms. Both imports and FDI exert competitive pressures on domestic firms, thereby increasing the incentives for domestic firms to innovate to survive in more competitive market conditions. Openness also encourages a more active

---

[38]See the recent literature reviews by Saggi (2006) and Smeets (2008) on research on FDI spillovers.

Figure 3.10   Openness to Trade, 2001–08

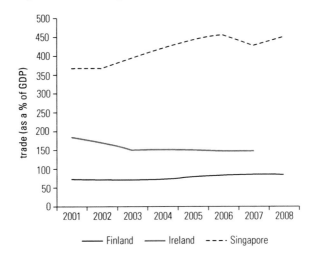

Source: World Bank's World Development Indicators database.

participation in the global market for technology through direct sales and purchases of technologies by domestic firms. Technology absorption and its global circulation are increasingly supported by investments in ICT infrastructure that contribute to connectivity, stimulate business activity, and raise productivity and innovativeness.

Openness to Trade and FDI

Small, open economies that rely on trade to sustain growth and openness have been a key to Sifire's success. Singapore, an entrepôt, tops the charts with trade as a share of GDP reaching 450 percent in 2008 (see figure 3.10). Ireland protected its domestic producers against U.K. imports from the 1930s through the mid-1960s.[39] This situation changed after Ireland signed the Anglo-Irish Free Trade Area Agreement in 1965 (Ruane and Görg 1999). The process of tariff reductions continued once Ireland joined the European Economic Community and was completed in 1978 (Rios-Morales and Brennan 2009; Ruane and Görg 1999). Its trade-to-GDP ratio was 150 percent in 2007. Finland also has been an open economy, with a

---

[39]During that period, FDI was prohibited by the Control of Manufactured Products Act. However, firms (especially U.K. firms) that were established before 1932, were allowed to continue their operations in Ireland. Hence, the act only limited the future inflow of FDI. Restrictions on FDI were abandoned once it became apparent that protected domestic manufacturing industries were failing to grow (Ruane and Görg 1999).

Figure 3.11   Imports of Goods and Services, 2001–08

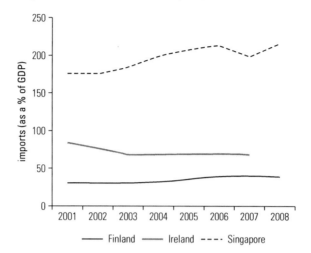

Source: World Bank's World Development Indicators database.

trade-to-GDP ratio of 84 percent in 2008. Imports of goods and services as a share of GDP were 215 percent, 69 percent, and 40 percent, respectively, in Singapore, Ireland, and Finland (see figure 3.11).

Singapore has traditionally relied on FDI as a key instrument of industrialization. On average, Singapore has attracted FDI equivalent to about 12 percent of GDP since 1980 (see figure 3.12). FDI inflows to Ireland and Finland were much smaller until the late 1990s. Foreign investors started to show interest in Ireland as a viable destination from 1990 onward, with FDI booming between 1998 and 2002. After 2004, the net inflow dipped into negative territory, because of a substantial divesture in 2004 and 2005. FDI flows seem to have reversed course and become positive in 2007, but they fell off again following the onset of the financial crisis in 2008.

Ireland's strategy was to attract FDI in high-tech industries and to promote links to domestic firms, mainly with the help of tax incentives, so as to maximize technology spillovers and domestic value added.[40] From 1956 to 1980, MNCs

---

[40] Using data on manufacturing establishments in Ireland from 1972 to 2000, Barrios, Görg, and Strobl (2005) found that the effect of inward FDI on domestic industry was nonlinear. At the beginning, the competition effect dominated, with the result that the number of domestic firms declined as more foreign firms entered the sector. However, as the share

(continued on next page)

Figure 3.12   Net Foreign Direct Investment Flows, 1980–2008

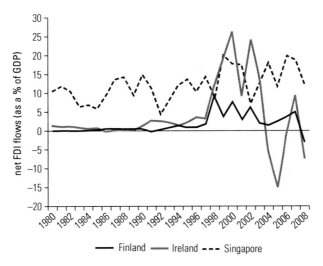

Source: World Bank's World Development Indicators database.

were exempted from the corporate income tax.[41] From 1980 to 2010, a 10 percent tax was applied on profits accruing from manufacturing, but only for those firms that were established before 1998. Since 2003, a corporate income tax of 12.5 percent has been levied on trading income, and a 25 percent rate applies to passive income and income from foreign trade. In addition, financial support is given in

---

(*continued from previous page*)
of MNCs increased, this trend seems to have had positive spillover on the net entry of domestic firms. For instance, MNCs dominated office machines and computers, accounting for 93 percent of all establishments in the sector from 1997 to 2000. However, this sector also had the highest net entry of domestic firms, averaging 17 percent between 1972 and 2000 (Barrios, Görg, and Strobl 2005). The longer MNCs were in Ireland, the more jobs they created. For every 100 jobs in MNCs, the local economy gained 100 additional jobs in services and 10 in manufacturing. The share of domestic purchases of raw materials and components by MNCs rose from 15 percent of their total purchases in the mid-1980s to 21 percent by 1997 and 24 percent for electronics firms (UNIDO 2005).

[41]Tax relief on exports profits was first introduced in 1956 (White 1983). This policy was initially set to end in 1990, but Ireland had to change the rule because of the complaints from the European Commission that the tax policy was against the Treaty of Rome (Ruane and Görg 1999).

the form of employment and training grants.[42] To promote inward FDI, Ireland established the Industrial Development Agency in the late 1960s.[43] Enterprise Ireland was established in 1993 to foster links between MNCs and local firms (Rios-Morales and Brennan 2009).[44]

Before 1997, FDI flows to Finland amounted to less than 1 percent of GDP. However, following the lifting of remaining restrictions on capital flows, Finland has begun attracting FDI, with flows peaking in 1998 at 7 percent of GDP. Since then, FDI inflows have fluctuated in the 3 to 5 percent range, becoming negative in 2008 because of the global slowdown.

Sifire countries have supplemented technology transfers embodied in imported equipment through FDI and through information flows with technology licensing. But unlike many other developing countries, they have skillfully extracted the maximum advantage because they have marshaled the scientific and network capital and assiduously built their manufacturing capabilities. Starting in the 1990s, Ireland has been actively acquiring foreign technologies, measured by royalty payments (see figure 3.13). Singapore also increased its acquisition of foreign technologies starting in the late 1990s. Finland, in contrast, has participated less actively in the purchase of technologies, although royalty payments began increasing in the 2000s. Royalty payments as a share of GDP also point to similar trend. Payments by Ireland and Singapore surged between the mid 1990s and the early 2000s (see figure 3.14).

ICT

All three economies perceived the long-term potential of ICT and focused on developing skill-intensive IT and telecommunication industries with the objective

---

[42]Interviews with MNCs from the United States reveal that the education of the workforce was the second most important factor in their decision to invest in Ireland (Barry 2007). (First was the low corporate income tax rate.) To persuade Intel to establish a production facility in Ireland, the Industrial Development Agency used every carrot and, to clinch the deal, commissioned interviews with 300 engineers of Irish origin (with the experience sought by Intel), most of whom were working in the United States. The Industrial Development Agency was able to convince Intel that 80 percent of the engineers would return to Ireland if offered an attractive job by a reputable company (Mac Sharry and White 2001). The importance of an educated workforce and the availability of good technical skills surface repeatedly in studies of the determinants of FDI. Costa Rica, for example, also used the promise of abundant skills as a lure for Intel (see Spar 1998).

[43]The 1969 Industrial Development Act created the present-day agency (White 1983).

[44]IDA's Linkage Program brought MNCs in contact with local firms and helped increase the multiplier effects of FDI.

Figure 3.13   Royalty Payments, 1975–2007

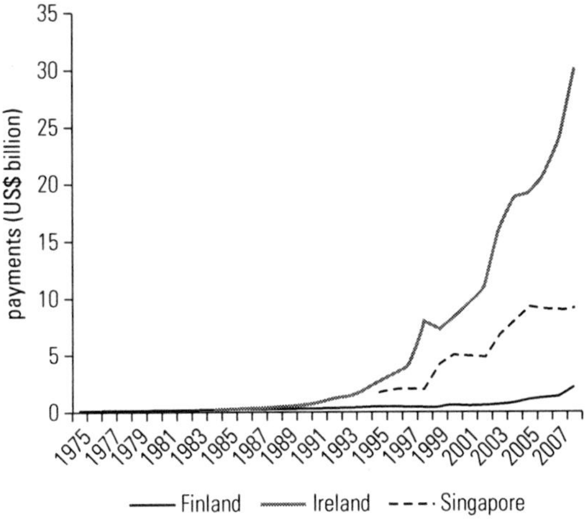

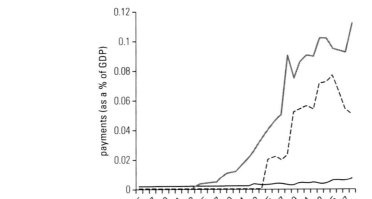

Source: World Bank's World Development Indicators database.

Figure 3.14   Royalty Payments as Share of GDP, 1975–2007

Source: World Bank's World Development Indicators database.

Table 3.38   Exports of ICT Goods, 1998–2006

Country	Share of total exports of goods (%)		
	1998	2002	2006
Finland	20.0	22.0	18.9
Ireland	29.0	30.8	22.4
Singapore	55.1	52.6	45.6

Source: World Bank's Information and Communications for Development database.

Table 3.39   Exports of ICT Services, 1998–2007

Country	Share of total exports of services (%)				
	1998	2000	2002	2004	2007
Finland	18.1	5.4	7.1	7.0	8.4
Ireland	33.7	45.5	38.2	36.4	30.1
Singapore	—	2.4	2.5	2.2	3.1

Source: World Bank's Information and Communications for Development database.
Note: — = not available.

of establishing a presence in the global market.[45] ICT-related products amounted to more than 40 percent of Singapore's total exports in 2006. The share of ICT-based exports was 22.4 percent in Ireland and 18.9 percent in Finland in the same year (see table 3.38). Ireland also excels in the export of ICT services. In 2007, close to one-third of services were related to ICT in Ireland (see table 3.39). The share of ICT-based services for Finland and Singapore are smaller: 8.4 percent and 3.1 percent, respectively.

Sifire's strength in exports of ICT goods and services is linked to the domestic investment in ICT infrastructure. From 2003 to 2008, Ireland, on average, spent more than 4 percent of its GDP on ICT; Finland spent more than 6 percent; and Singapore, more than 7 percent (see table 3.40).

---

[45]Investment in ICT contributed 0.6 to 0.8 percentage points to total factor productivity growth in Finland during 1995 to 2000 and 0.6 percentage points to Ireland's growth. See Honkapohja and others (2009). According to Atkinson and others (2010), the U.S. economy added US$1.6 trillion to its GDP between 1995 and 2006 on the strength of investment in and use of ICT. Every dollar invested by large firms in ICT increased the company's market value by US$25, with ICT workers (and capital) contributing far more to a firm's productivity than non-ICT workers. Korea also derived 20 percent of its growth from investment in ICT. Among the business models and processes linked to ICT are supply-chain management (raised to a fine art by Walmart), marketing of a wide range of products to benefit

(continued on next page)

Table 3.40   ICT Expenditure as a Share of GDP, 2003–08

Country	Share of GDP (%)					
	2003	2004	2005	2006	2007	2008
Finland	6.9	7.6	7.6	7.7	7.3	6.5
Ireland	4.9	4.9	4.8	4.8	4.5	4.6
Singapore	10.1	9.7	9.6	8.7	7.5	7.1

Source: World Bank's Information and Communications for Development database.

Table 3.41   Internet Users, 1995–2008

Country	Number of users per 100 people					
	1995	2000	2003	2005	2007	2008
Finland	13.9	37.2	65.9	72.6	79.0	82.5
Ireland	1.1	17.8	30.8	37.5	57.0	62.7
Singapore	2.8	32.3	54.4	61.9	67.7	69.6

Source: World Bank's Information and Communications for Development database.

As a result, the number of people in the Sifire countries who have Internet connections has increased tremendously. In 1995, only a handful of people had Internet connections in Ireland and Singapore, and even in Finland the figure was low (see table 3.41). Internet connections in Finland increased from 13.9 percent in 1995 to 72.6 percent in 2005, and in Singapore, from 2.8 percent to 61.9 percent. The diffusion of the Internet was slower in Ireland, with the penetration rate in 2005 only about half of Finland's rate. By 2008, at 62.7 percent, Ireland was approaching Singapore but was still well behind Finland.

Noteworthy also is the speed of broadband diffusion in these countries. In Singapore, almost all Internet users were connected by broadband by 2008 (see table 3.42). Similarly, for Ireland, 79 percent of Internet users were using broadband connection. Although recent figures for Finland are not available, it would be safe to assume that broadband represents the vast majority of connections.

(continued from previous page)
from the "long tail" (as is practiced by Amazon), more sophisticated pricing models, self-service kiosks, mass customization (a specialty of Dell), IT-enabled service, and collaborative design and innovation. InnoCentive, for example, has used crowd sourcing to garner solutions to scientific problems, and is one of the leading practitioners of the open, contest- and prize-based approach to innovation that is now attracting much attention. For more information, see Travis (2008) and Hotz (2009). On the contribution of ICT to growth in OECD countries, see Jorgenson, Ho, and Stiroh (2005, 2008) and van Ark, Inklaar, and McGuckin (2003).

Table 3.42   Fixed Broadband Subscribers, 2000–08

Country	Share of total Internet subscribers (%)							
	2000	**2001**	**2002**	**2003**	**2004**	**2005**	**2006**	**2008**
Finland	5.7	14.1	25.9	37.3	57.1	—	—	—
Ireland	0.0	—	1.0	3.5	18.6	34.8	57.6	79.0
Singapore	8.1	7.8	13.4	19.0	24.3	29.1	34.1	90.9

Source: World Bank's Information and Communications for Development database.
Note: — = not available.

Table 3.43   International Internet Bandwidth, 1999–2007

Country	Bits per second per person		
	1999	**2003**	**2007**
Finland	129.7	3,463.7	17,220.6
Ireland	63.6	5,040.2	15,228.6
Singapore	213.5	3,782.4	22,783.4

Source: World Bank's Information and Communications for Development database.

With high investment in ICT infrastructure, the Sifire countries also increased their connectivity to other countries. In fewer than 10 years, the international Internet bandwidth available to each person increased more than 100-fold (see table 3.43). High connectivity to other countries is essential if the Sifire group wishes to remain competitive in both manufacturing and IT-enabled services. And it is vital for international networking, which is increasingly the lifeblood of open innovation systems.

Concluding Observations

Sifire successfully managed the economic transition from primary- and resource-based production systems to more high-tech economic structures. All three countries did so by leveraging technological advances in key subsectors with the rise of advances in electronics and telecommunication (from fixed line to mobile), thereby opening new industrial pathways. Globalization in general—and for Finland and Ireland, integration with the EU—widened market opportunities that were essential for their industrial development. Without access to large external markets, these small countries would not have been able to grow as rapidly and consistently as they have done.

More important, they were able to anticipate the changes in economic structure, match the upcoming labor demand with quality education, and capitalize on the externalities inherent in networking. Sifire first focused on providing universal primary education and expanded secondary and tertiary education as demand for higher skills began rising. High levels of enrollment in the science and engineering fields enabled the Sifire countries to accelerate industrialization and assisted in the progressive upgrading of new and traditional industries.

References

Aarrevaara, Timo, Ian R. Dobson, and Camilla Elander. 2009. "Brave New World: Higher Education Reform in Finland." *Higher Education Management and Policy* 21 (2): 87–104.

Atkinson, Robert D., Stephen J. Ezell, Scott M. Andes, Daniel D. Castro, and Richard Bennett. 2010. *The Internet Economy 25 Years after .Com: Transforming Commerce and Life*. Washington, DC: Information Technology and Innovation Foundation. http://www.itif.org/files/2010-25-years.pdf.

Barrios, Salvador, Holger Görg, and Eric Strobl. 2005. "Foreign Direct Investment, Competition, and Industrial Development in the Host Country." *European Economic Review* 49 (7): 1761–84.

Barro, Robert J., and Jong-Wee Lee. 2000. "International Data on Educational Attainment: Updates and Implications." CID Working Paper 042, Center for International Development, Harvard University, Cambridge, MA.

Barry, Frank. 2007. "The Most FDI-Intensive Economy in Europe: Analysis of the Irish Experience and Current Policy Issues." In *Foreign Direct Investment in Europe: A Changing Landscape*, ed. Klaus Liebscher, Josef Christl, Peter Mooslechner, and Doris Ritzberger-Gruenwald, 247–57. Cheltenham, U.K.: Edward Elgar.

Bloom, David, and David Canning. 2003. "Contraception and the Celtic Tiger." *Economic and Social Review* 34 (3): 229–247.

Crafts, Nicholas. 2005. "Interpreting Ireland's Economic Growth." Background report for the United Nations Industrial Development Organization's *Industrial Development Report 2005: Capability Building for Catching-Up—Historical, Empirical, and Policy Dimensions*, Vienna, Austria.

Dahlman, Carl J., Jorma Routti, and Pekka Ylä-Anttila. 2007. *Finland as a Knowledge Economy: Elements of Success and Lessons Learned*. Washington, DC: World Bank.

Daveri, Francesco, and Olmo Silva. 2004. "Not Only Nokia: What Finland Tells Us about New Economy Growth." *Economic Policy* 19 (38): 117–63.

Department of Statistics. Various years. *Yearbook of Statistics Singapore*. Singapore: Ministry of Trade and Industry.

Fallon, Ivan. 2007. "Luck and the Irish, by RF Foster: Why Irish Eyes Are Smiling." *Independent*, November 16. http://www.independent.co.uk/arts-entertainment/books/reviews/luck-and-the-irish-by-rf-foster-400487.html.

Goh, Chor Boon, and S. Gopinathan. 2008. "Education in Singapore: Developments Since 1965." In *An African Exploration of the East Asian Education Experience*, ed. Birger Fredriksen and Jee Peng Tan, 80–108. Washington, DC: World Bank.

Häikiö, Martti. 2002. *Nokia: The Inside Story*. London: FT Prentice Hall.

Honkapohja, Seppo, Erkki A. Koskela, Willi Leibfritz, and Roope Uusitalo. 2009. *Economic Prosperity Recaptured: The Finnish Path from Crisis to Rapid Growth*. Cambridge, MA: MIT Press.

Honohan, Patrick, and Brendan Walsh. 2002. "Catching Up with the Leaders: The Irish Hare." *Brookings Papers on Economic Activity* 33 (1): 1–78.

Hotz, Robert Lee. 2009. "The Science Prize: Innovation or Stealth Advertising?" *Wall Street Journal*, May 8.

Jorgenson, Dale W., Mun S. Ho, and Kevin J. Stiroh. 2005. "Growth of U.S. Industries and Investments in Information Technology and Higher Education." In *Measuring Capital in the New Economy*, ed. Carol Corrado, John Haltiwanger, and Daniel Sichel, 403–78. Chicago: University of Chicago Press.

———. 2008. "A Retrospective Look at the U.S. Productivity Growth Resurgence." *Journal of Economic Perspectives* 22 (1): 3–24.

Kearns, Allan, and Frances Ruane. 2001. "The Tangible Contribution of R&D Spending Foreign-Owned Plants to a Host Region: A Plant Level Study of the Irish Manufacturing Sector (1980–1996)." *Research Policy* 30 (2): 227–44.

Kis, Viktória. 2010. "Learning for Jobs: OECD Reviews of Vocational Education and Training—Ireland." Organisation for Economic Co-operation and Development, Paris.

Lester, Richard K. 2005. "Universities, Innovation, and the Competitiveness of Local Economies: Summary Report from the Local Innovation Project—Phase I." MIT-IPC Working Paper 05-010, Industrial Performance Center, Massachusetts Institute of Technology, Cambridge, MA.

Mac Sharry, Ray, and Padraic White. 2001. *The Making of the Celtic Tiger: The Inside Story of Ireland's Boom Economy*. Cork, Ireland: Mercier.

Martin, M. O., I. V. S. Mullis, and P. Foy. 2008. Chestnut Hill, MA: TIMMS and PIRLS International Study Center, Boston College.

Migration News. 2006. "UK, Ireland." *Migration News* 13 (2). http://migration.ucdavis.edu/mn/more.php?id=3186_0_4_0.

Mullis, I. V. S., M. O. Martin, and P. Foy. 2008. Chestnut Hill, MA: TIMMS and PIRLS International Study Center, Boston College.

Nabeshima, Kaoru. 2004. "Technology Transfer in East Asia: A Survey." In *Global Production Networking and Technological Change in East Asia*, ed. Shahid Yusuf, M. Anjum Altaf, and Kaoru Nabeshima, 395–434. New York: Oxford University Press.

OECD (Organisation for Economic Co-operation and Development). 2000. *Economic Surveys: Finland*. Paris: OECD.

———. 2003. *Polytechnic Education in Finland*. Paris: OECD.

———. 2006. *Review of Innovation Policy: Switzerland*. Paris: OECD.

———. 2009. *PISA 2009 Results: What Students Know and Can Do*. Paris: OECD.

———. 2010. *Strong Performers and Successful Reformers in Education: Lessons from PISA for the United States*. Paris: OECD.

Ojala, Jari, Jari Eloranta, and Jukka Jalava, eds. 2006. *The Road to Prosperity: An Economic History of Finland*. Helsinki: Suomalaisen Kirjallisuuden Seura.

O'Toole, Fintan. 2009. *Ship of Fools: How Stupidity and Corruption Sank the Celtic Tiger.* London: Faber and Faber.

Rios-Morales, Ruth, and Louis Brennan. 2009. "Ireland's Innovative Governmental Policies Promoting Internationalisation." *Research in International Business and Finance* 23 (2): 157–68.

Ruane, Frances, and Holger Görg. 1999. "Irish FDI Policy and Investment from the EU." In *Innovation, Investment, and the Diffusion of Technology in Europe*, ed. Ray Barrell and Nigel Pain, 44–67. Cambridge, U.K.: Cambridge University Press.

Saarinen, Jani. 2005. *Innovations and Industrial Performance in Finland, 1945–1998.* Stockholm: Almqvist & Wiksell International.

Saggi, Kamal. 2006. "Foreign Direct Investment, Linkages, and Technology Spillovers." In *Global Integration and Technology Transfer*, ed. Bernard Hoekman and Beata Smarzynska Javorcik, 51–65. Washington, DC: World Bank.

Shanmugaratnam, Tharman. 2009. "Investing in a Knowledge Based Society: East Asia's Experience." Address at the Conference for African Ministers of Finance and Education: Sustaining Education Gains Amidst the Global Economic Crisis, Tunis, July 15–17.

Smeets, Roger. 2008. "Collecting the Pieces of the FDI Knowledge Spillovers Puzzle." *World Bank Research Observer* 23 (2): 107–38.

Spar, Debora. 1998. "Attracting High Technology Investment: Intel's Costa Rican Plant." Washington, DC. FIAS Occasional Paper 11, Foreign Investment Advisory Service, World Bank, Washington, DC.

Travis, John. 2008. "Science by the Masses." *Science* 319 (5871): 1750–52.

UNIDO (United Nations Industrial Development Organization). 2005. *Industrial Development Report 2005: Capability Building for Catching-Up—Historical, Empirical, and Policy Dimensions.* Vienna, Austria: UNIDO.

van Ark, Bart, Robert Inklaar, and Robert H. McGuckin. 2003. "The Contribution of ICT-Producing and ICT-Using Industries to Productivity Growth: A Comparison of Canada, Europe, and the United States." *International Productivity Monitor* 6 (Spring): 56–63.

White, Padraic A. 1983. "A Concept of Industrial Development in the 1980s." *Journal of the Statistical and Social Inquiry Society of Ireland* 24 (5): 51–59.

Yeoh, Brenda S. A. 2007. "Singapore: Hungry for Foreign Workers at All Skill Levels." *Migration Information Source*, January. http://www.migrationinformation.org/Profiles/display.cfm?ID=570.

Ylä-Anttila, Pekka. 2007. "Finland's Knowledge Economy Today." In *Finland as a Knowledge Economy: Elements of Success and Lessons Learned*, ed. Carl Dahlman, Jorma Routti, and Pekka Ylä-Anttila, 9–16. Washington, DC: World Bank.

Ylä-Anttila, Pekka, and Christopher Palmberg. 2007. "Economic and Industrial Policy Transformations in Finland." *Journal of Industry Competition and Trade* 7 (3–4): 169–87.

4

Governance and Growth

Theories of endogenous growth have pointed to the growth-inducing effects of technological externalities, or spillovers, arising from the accumulation of human capital. But experience has taught us that realizing the sought-after growth is not just a matter of increased spending on education and research. Growth can help build the human capital and research infrastructure, but the externalities may not follow. Here the inexact science of institutions comes into play. Institutions provide a matrix of the rules and organizations to guide the accumulation of resources along with their allocation and use. With stronger, better-designed institutions, countries can arrive at superior outcomes. Where institutions are weak or mostly informal, economic activities can be severely constrained, with interpersonal transactions predominating. Worse still, ineffective or missing institutions or ones that lead to dysfunctional behavior can be welfare subtracting. Once entrenched, institutions with dysfunctional behavior are difficult to rectify and erase, thereby making it harder for organizations and individuals to engage in activities requiring complex and long-term contracts underpinned by mechanisms for effective enforcement. Moreover, distorted rules and corrupt organizations generate perverse incentives.

A large literature, using a variety of proxies, has attempted to demonstrate the relationships between institutions and growth with some success, although doubts remain. Many of those doubts arise from the choice of explanatory variables and the econometric tests used. However, with regard to the Sifire group, a robust case can be made that governance institutions had a big hand in building human capital and in augmenting spillovers.

The term *institution* can refer to a set of rules affecting behavior, and it can also refer to an organization. An important category of institutions affects governance. A definition proposed by Avinash Dixit (2009, 5) is illuminating. According to Dixit, economic governance is "the structure and functioning of the legal and social institutions that support economic activity and economic transactions by protecting property rights, enforcing contracts, and taking collective action to provide physical and organizational infrastructure." Whether economic governance promotes growth is a function of the commitment and credibility of the government and the primacy it attaches to economic results; the quality of the organizational infrastructure responsible for planning, administering, and coordinating development; and the implementation capability of key public and private entities that are engaged in resource mobilization, allocation, production, and technological change.

A leadership that sets its sights on effectively harnessing technology for development can initiate a virtuous spiral, and, as was argued earlier, a crisis can catalyze such determined action.[1] But when governance institutions are weak, the process of accumulating and deepening technology can be slow to gather momentum or can fail altogether. The nature of the institutional base can have a strong bearing on the development of organizational capability, which is the handmaiden of economic performance. The state need not play the lead role in providing governance as a part of its public function; private parties can also do so. However, as Dixit observes, "In most countries, we find a mixture of the formal legal system and a rich and complex array of informal social institutions of governance. These mixtures reflect the country's level of economic development and in turn help to determine its economic prospects" (Dixit 2007b, 3; see also Dixit 2007a).

The Sifire countries were fortunate in that during the decades before the 1980s governance institutions were able to mature, and these mature institutions helped strengthen the organizational capabilities of the state.

In each case, institutional efficacy and sustained growth was spearheaded by a major government entity vested with substantial authority. It is also notable that the economic system as a whole could respond speedily to the stimuli provided. Education and training could be ramped up, the physical and research infrastructure expanded, and the business community galvanized to work closely with other parts of the economy to realize ambitious growth objectives. This chapter shows how the Funding Agency for Technology and Innovation (Tekes) in Finland, the Industrial Development Agency (IDA) in Ireland, and the Economic Development Board (EDB) in Singapore helped to plan and implement effective strategies once the commitment to growth and the necessity of yoking it to knowledge and human capital had been resolved (on EDB's achievements see Chan 2011).

By the 1980s, the three countries had developed the basic institutional ecosystem of a modern economy, with well-staffed and well-functioning organizations. Sifire shared these characteristics with many other industrializing countries, but in making the system deliver results, Sifire proved to be a cut or several cuts above the rest.

---

[1] See Kanbur (2009) for a recent view on crises and the proposition that recurrent crises might be the new normal.

The vulnerability of small countries surrounded by more populous and prosperous neighbors can help to focus national attention on competitiveness in the interests of achieving comparable living standards.[2] Small countries can be readier to mobilize domestic resources, and when they have few resources, the value of human capital is more apparent. Also, small economies are quicker to realize that domestic supplies and markets must be supplemented by resources from abroad and access to foreign markets. Thus, the more enterprising small economies are oriented outward and have a strong sense of how their fortunes are linked with those of the regional economy and, in recent decades, to those of the global economy as well. They can see how their future depends on close interaction with other countries at many different levels to augment their narrow base of capital, labor, skills, and ideas and to tap external market opportunities.

Interaction with other countries on terms advantageous to small economies depends on competitiveness—the creation of a business environment that is attractive to foreign investors; of cities that offer services, amenities, and lifestyles that will pull in tourists and long-stay knowledge workers; and of specialized technologies and skills for producing differentiated and quality manufactures and services. Such countries must also have the agility to keep one step ahead of other economies by diversifying into activities with greater potential as returns from existing activities begin to erode. To consistently deliver results in each of these areas over many years is a tall order. However, Sifire countries have proved more adept than most other small economies. And their innovation in managing development must be given a major share of the credit.

The starting point for each of the three countries was a leadership that forged a consensus on economic objectives and the means for achieving them. Such leadership is most apparent in the case of Singapore, where Lee Kuan Yew was the undisputed and justly admired driving force, and his party, the People's Action Party (PAP), dominated and continues to dominate the polls.[3] To lesser degrees, the broad strategy pursued by the political leadership in Finland and Ireland buttressed institutional and organizational capabilities. In Ireland, the Fianna Fáil government was able to achieve common cause with the opposition Fine Gael

---

[2]A comparison between Jamaica and Singapore by Lerner (2009) reminds us that too few countries have risen to the challenge. When they gained independence in 1965, the two countries were comparable in populations and per capita gross domestic products (GDPs)—US$2,650 versus US$2,850. But four decades later, Singapore had a per capita GDP of US$31,400 while Jamaica had a per capita GDP of US$4,800. Lerner lists various factors that weighed in Singapore's favor, such as governance, human capital, and macrostability, but gives special importance to entrepreneurship, which he believes Singapore was far more successful in inculcating.

[3]Lee Kuan Yew resigned his cabinet position as minister mentor on May 14, 2011, following elections that saw the PAP's share of the popular vote decline to 60.1 percent.

Party and enter a social partnership with businesses and labor by adopting a conciliatory and cooperative approach (*Economist* 2004; Honohan and Walsh 2002).[4] Labor was willing to accept wage restraint in exchange for more policy influence because unions were weakened by the huge increase in unemployment in the mid 1980s. The result was the resumption of a policy dialogue among the principal stakeholders and the forging of what Seán O'Riain has called the "flexible development state" to differentiate it from the more bureaucratic development states in East Asia (O'Riain 2000, 158). Unemployment approaching 20 percent in the early 1990s also helped build a political consensus in Finland around a knowledge-based strategy. This consensus was bolstered institutionally by the Finnish parliament's creation of the Committee for the Future in 1993 to conduct a dialogue with the government to find solutions for emerging problems. Such leadership and its continuity allowed a vision to be shaped and long-term programs to be initiated and implemented. As these examples illustrate, rather than being held hostage to short-term political exigencies and vicissitudes, the Sifire countries were able to work steadily toward longer-term objectives.

A leadership committed to a firm economic agenda that enjoyed broad support could strengthen the economic governance institutions and deepen the organizational capabilities to enforce rules, uphold the law, and frame as well as implement policies. In fact, it was in the area of organizational capabilities that Sifire countries were innovative and able to establish new benchmarks of excellence.

Few would question the efficacy of the market mechanism in allocating resources and incentivizing production. But few also would deny that markets are myopic and can fail to coordinate the actions of multiple participants, especially when such coordination needs to be orchestrated over a period of years. Markets cannot easily accommodate scale economies and externalities. The Sifire countries are all market economies; however, the governments in these countries realized that to run ahead of the pack they would need more than what the markets alone could deliver. The crises of the 1980s added to the urgency of taking measures to avoid stagnation. The answer seemed to lie in creating organizational capabilities that could help to enlarge the information set of current or prospective market participants, to contain risks, to sweeten incentives for certain activities with perceived long-term potential, and to work to coordinate the actions of various parties whose joint effort was necessary to realize longer-term objectives.

Coordinators

Small economies have an advantage in that they can set their sights lower and seek simpler solutions that are frugal in the use of resources. The Sifire group needed

---

[4]The corporatist Irish approach was in marked contrast to the confrontational strategy adopted by Margaret Thatcher's government in the United Kingdom.

to define a route to a more knowledge-intensive economy with solid long-term growth prospects. Transparent and effective governance institutions were the necessary foundations of such an economy. And to complement those institutions, governments needed organizations with the authority and capabilities to take a long-term perspective and implement policies promptly.[5] Each country adopted a two-pronged approach of streamlining governance and market institutions and entrusting a single agency with the task of delivering the key elements of a growth strategy. Other economic agencies were also structured to support the lead strategic agency and ensure the integrity of the governance institutions.

To promote the development of indigenous technologies that would contribute to the competitiveness of Finnish firms, the government of Finland established Tekes in 1983 to stimulate technology development and to encourage innovation. Tekes has a broad and ambitious mandate to look ahead and identify the promising areas for technological advance—including industrial diversification—and to coordinate the working of the innovation system with the help of catalytic funding of research and development (R&D). (See figure 4.1, which presents the main components of the Finnish innovation system.) Tekes is guided by the Research and Innovation Council (known as the Science and Technology Policy Council prior to 2009). Tekes is chaired by the prime minister[6] and works closely with government agencies; with the Academy of Finland, which promotes basic research; with Sitra (the Finnish Innovation Fund); and with universities, firms, and private financiers.[7] Tekes pushes the government's innovation agenda and attempts to keep Finland at the leading edge of technological change in selected areas of specialization. With a budget of €500 million provided by the Ministry of Trade and Industry, Tekes has financed up to 2,000 projects annually—mostly R&D activities undertaken by firms, but a quarter or more are initiated by universities and other research bodies.

Tekes's role in the renaissance of Finnish technology is widely recognized. By combining strategic foresight on fruitful areas for medium-term R&D with networking and coordination skills and implementation capacity, this modestly scaled agency with a staff of 400 (about a fifth of whom are stationed in the leading

---

[5]Hung (2000, 199) notes that the institutional environment most conducive to industrial development comprises a policy network embracing all public agencies concerned with industrial issues, a business system that encourages firms to establish relationships with each other, and a technology institution to "trigger social dynamics, develop technology paradigms, and define innovation directions."

[6]A recent report on the Finnish innovation system has called for greater involvement by the Prime Minister's Office in making innovation policy. Such efforts, the report states, should go beyond the chairing of the Research and Innovation Council by the prime minister (Ministry of Education and Ministry of Employment and the Economy 2009).

[7]Greater collaboration between universities and industry has been one of Tekes's policy imperatives (Srinivas and Viljamaa 2003).

Figure 4.1 Finnish Innovation System: Organizations and Coordination

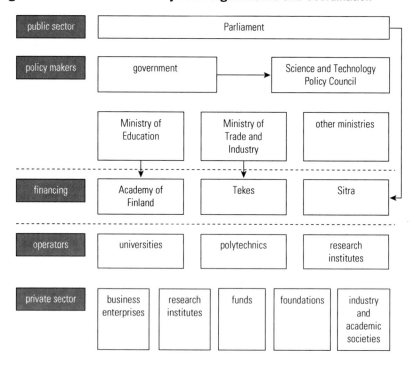

Source: Dahlman, Routti, and Ylä-Anttila 2006.

Organisation for Economic Co-operation and Development countries) has made Finland one of the world's most innovative nations and has fueled its growth for almost two decades. Tekes added value, not just by providing low-interest loans and grants for research, but also by expanding information channels and increasing information flows. It did so by developing international contacts and collaborative links with talented research teams in Finland and abroad and by convening seminars, study visits, and training programs.

Sitra, founded in 1967 by the Bank of Finland with an endowment of FIM 100 million (approximately €700 million), morphed into a venture capital fund in the 1980s and helped pioneer venture capitalism. However, over the past decade, Sitra, which is independent of government control and has the leeway to engage in experimentation and to attempt to fix networking failures, has redefined its mission to complement the activities of other parts of the innovation system. Sitra now sees its role as looking ahead, coming up with ideas for future urban lifestyles, and helping to design models of service delivery by working closely with private companies and other stakeholders. One example is the Low2No project in the Helsinki harbor area, a low-carbon initiative that is attempting to pilot a new approach to urban design. Sitra's objective, like that of other similar organizations in Sweden (Vinnova) and Denmark (MindLab), is to encourage forward thinking and fuel innovation by catalyzing ideas and supporting commercial initiatives through partnerships and cofinancing (Ministry of Education and Ministry of Employment and the Economy 2009, 25).

Ireland's Industrial Development Agency was established as a branch of the Department of Industry and Commerce in 1949. When Ireland began casting around for a growth strategy with a focus on foreign direct investment (FDI) by multinationals, IDA emerged as the lead agency to target potential investors and market Ireland's institutional advantages, location, and human resources. (See figure 4.2 for the organizational configuration of the Irish innovation system.)

IDA's strategy, similar to that of Tekes, is grounded in Ireland's perceived areas of comparative advantage—current or prospective—and is aimed at attracting investment into niches that could potentially house dynamic industrial clusters.

To interest investors, IDA worked closely with Irish providers of infrastructure and skills. Bringing urban infrastructure services to world-class levels was one of the agency's principal objectives. Improving and expanding the technical and soft skills of the Irish workforce was a second objective. Progress in these areas was vital to the success of IDA's efforts at persuading multinational corporations (MNCs) to establish production and research facilities in Ireland and to house their regional headquarters in Dublin. Such progress was also essential to persuade MNCs and other firms to steadily upgrade their activities so as to pull the Irish economy higher up the value chain. IDA's efforts were reinforced by the Science Foundation of Ireland, which was created in 2000 to manage the €646 million Technology Foresight Fund. The fund's purpose was to multiply the ties between the research and business communities in conjunction with the Programme for Research in Third-Level Institutions (UNIDO 2005, 81).

In 2009, IDA's expenditures amounted to €230 million, derived mostly from the exchequer and supplemented with funds from the European Union (EU) and sales of property (IDA 2009). The relatively modest outlay built organizational capabilities that enabled Ireland to emerge from obscurity to become the Celtic tiger economy, viewed as the equal of some of the East Asian economies, in a matter of two decades.

Singapore's EDB, a statutory body formed in 1961, is the oldest of the three agencies and, arguably, has the strongest track record (figure 4.3). From as early as the 1960s, it was apparent to Singapore's leaders that to thrive, the city-state needed a steady flow of FDI. Although its location was an enduring asset, Singapore could secure prosperity only by crafting a near-ideal business environment and the best-trained workforce in Southeast Asia. EDB's mission was to engineer an efficient and low-transaction-cost environment and to work with other agencies and the education system to raise the quality of Singapore's labor. Much like Tekes, EDB has looked ahead, consulted widely, and planned strategically with an

108

Figure 4.2 Irish Science and Technology Structures

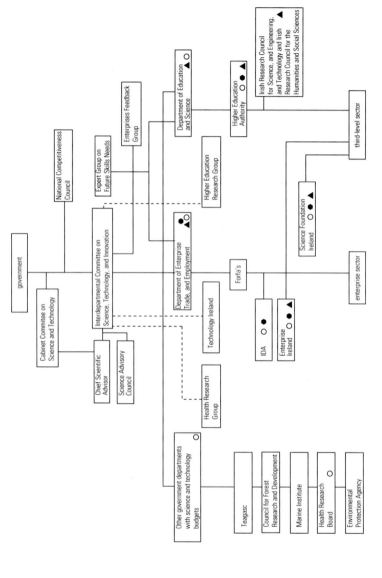

Technology Ireland member organization
Higher Education Research Group member organization
Health Research Group member organization

Source: EU Community Research and Development Information Service (http://cordis.europa.eu).

Figure 4.3   The EDB Network

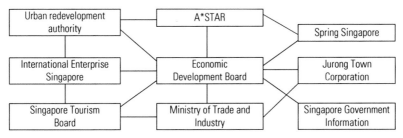

Source: EDB Singapore and Kumar and Siddique 2010.

eye to the likely maturing and migration of existing industries and the need to replace them with industries further up the value chain. Each shock or crisis has further underscored the need for strategic thinking and a rapid response. EDB's experience has demonstrated how well-resourced and experienced organizations with implementation skills can help a small economy forge ahead industrially in a highly competitive global environment by charting a strategy, serving as an interface between MNCs and local agencies, and acting to realize evolving strategic objectives by coordinating the delivery of skills, services, and capital to meet anticipated industrial demand. Singapore's smoothly functioning economy is a tribute to EDB's farsightedness and the intangible capital accumulated by this elite body.

Institutions for Growth

Sifire's experience with institutions and development agencies illuminates and lends current relevance to the lessons that emerged from the Industrial Revolution in Great Britain and that have been repeatedly reinforced in a variety of contexts. Institutions safeguarding property—physical and intellectual—and enforcing contracts have received due recognition. But technological advances, both radical and incremental, which are so integral to the process of development, have been significantly reinforced by other institutions.[8] These institutions go a long way toward explaining the rapidity with which the Sifire countries were able to exploit technological possibilities and are available to other low- and lower-middle-income countries eager to harness the technologies that will unlatch the door to greater prosperity.

Historians of science have underscored the importance of institutions that encouraged and gave prominence to learning and to accretion of usable knowledge—what

---

[8]Rodrik, Subramanian, and Trebbi (2002) maintain that quality institutions trump other determinants of growth.

Joel Mokyr (2002) has labeled "propositional knowledge"—about how nature works. The elaboration of this modern scientific knowledge was the province initially of relatively small numbers of thinkers and discoverers, mainly in Europe,[9] and, as we come closer to the present, of an international army of scientists, technologists, engineers, and creative workers. The contribution of scientific knowledge and modern technologies to standards of living and the quality of life are now well understood, but many countries have failed to create the institutions to accumulate the knowledge capital that is the necessary stepping-stone to technological advances. Such accumulation derives from the significance a society attaches to usable knowledge and to technological innovation of manifold kinds. It derives from the ways capital is built with the help of learned bodies; from incentives for and recognition of technological prowess; from the resources and effort a society devotes to improving the quality of education at all levels; from investment in research universities, think-tanks, and other institutes of learning; and from the garnering of a scientific culture in cities by staging events that engage people from all walks of life and that, in particular, captivate the imagination of the young.

The accumulation of knowledge capital can be severely handicapped in the absence of institutions that render a society open to new ideas from within and from other countries. Two centuries ago, when scientific activity tended to be more localized and the pace of change was slower, whether a society was open barely mattered. Now that a large number of countries are contributing to the scientific edifice and technological advance is a global pursuit, openness is vital not just to maximize the absorption of findings from elsewhere but also to allow the greatest freedom in how the fund of knowledge is to be manipulated, how new

---

[9]Meisenzahl and Mokyr (2011) maintain that the British industrial revolution was the work of a small number of inventors, who were aided by the practical knowledge and innovativeness of a multitude of skilled craftworkers. Although Arabic science contributed substantially to mathematical, methodological, and scientific knowledge and, until the 14th century, was far ahead of science in Europe, Huff (1993, 62, 63) is correct in observing that it "failed to give birth to modern science," and "Arabic-Islamic civilization did not succeed in its march toward the development of this universal institution of modernity." Huff (1993, 67) continues, "The rise of modern science was not just the triumph of technical reasoning but an intellectual struggle over the constitution of the legitimating directive structures of the West.... Intellectually, modern science represents a new canon of proof and evidence; institutionally, it represents a new configuration of role structures." Shapin (1996, 164) makes a similar point when he remarks that "the more a body of knowledge is understood to be objective and disinterested, the more valuable it is as a tool in moral and political action.... That paradox is also a legacy of the Scientific Revolution, when disengaged scholars and gentlemen forged a body of knowledge that was enormously useful for theology and politics precisely because its practitioners advertised the boundaries between science and the affairs of the church and the state."

combinations will be tried, and how new ideas will be explored with globalization. The tendrilous reaching of the World Wide Web to the farthest corners of the world and the openness supported by protocols and rules governing web-based communication have rendered societies more porous than ever before. Knowledge flows more freely than at any time in the past. That this freedom is not seen in some quarters as an unalloyed good is also evident from the steps being taken in some countries to police the Internet. Nevertheless, the universe of knowledge and the dynamics of knowledge flows and accumulation have been transformed. On average, smaller resource-poor countries that are more dependent on close interaction and commerce with other nations have tended toward greater openness. For them, the shortest path to the accumulation of knowledge capital is to augment domestic investment in such capital by opening their windows and letting it stream in.

Openness enlarges access to knowledge, but the efficient gathering of knowledge, its use, and the sparking of fresh ideas require the piecing together of networks. As the quantum of knowledge in every field has deepened and individuals have inevitably become more specialized, technology development, fresh discoveries, and problem solving of all sorts require greater teamwork (Adams 2004). Fewer technical papers are written by a single author as the complexity of products and services has risen, and the need for cross-disciplinary efforts has become essential in many cases. Not infrequently, novel solutions to knotty problems come from individuals or teams working on widely separated research.

Power of Urban Networks

Small countries, where most of the population is concentrated in a few cities or, in the case of Singapore, a single city, enjoy the advantages of productivity augmenting agglomeration (see Glaeser and Resseger 2009), ease of personal interaction, and—potentially—the creation of horizontal ties that germinate social capital. A high degree of ethnic and cultural homogeneity can further assist the process by contributing to the formation of social capital.[10] With one-third of Ireland's population located in Dublin and one-third of Finland's population living in Helsinki[11] and in two neighboring cities of Espoo and Turku,[12] the demographic

---

[10]See Putnam (2007) on the effects of ethnic diversity on trust and the formation of social capital.

[11]The Helsinki metropolitan area includes the cities of Espoo, Vantaa, and Kauniainen. A quarter of all Finns live in the Helsinki region, and eight of Finland's 20 universities are located there, as are 70 percent of foreign companies with operations in Finland.

[12]Turku, the former capital of the Grand Duchy of Finland, has built nutraceutical and pharmaceutical (therapeutic) businesses on the foundations provided by a food industry (Srinivas and Viljamaa 2003).

center of gravity in both countries is clearly demarcated. Each of the three countries has a dominant ethnic majority that sets the cultural tone and puts its stamp on social institutions. Finland and Ireland were ethnically more homogeneous in the 1980s than was Singapore, and although both countries have absorbed large numbers of immigrants since, they remain less diverse.

Urban demographics, "thick" sociocultural norms, and plentiful social capital are the foundations for networking. Through the 1990s, they have been reinforced by the diffusion of technologies that have enormously increased electronic communication and have stimulated greater face-to-face interaction in the urban environment.[13] Networking builds on trust, and once networks jell, bonds are tested, and members gain in confidence, trust-based relationships grow stronger. Such connectedness and multistranded relationships are notable features of urban societies in Sifire, and it is important to understand how they have supported development.

Recall that in the 1980s, Finland, Ireland, and Singapore were middle-income countries, had already attained a measure of technological capability, and had established manufacturing bases. They were equipped to assimilate codified technologies and needed to move beyond to begin absorbing the less codified or uncodified tacit knowledge on which depended the mastering of frontier technologies. Making this leap required trust-based networking that created the channels for sharing knowledge and encouraged collective effort at refining and extending this knowledge. In the process, new intellectual vistas and commercial opportunities would open.[14]

Networking served other purposes also. Sifire countries needed to mobilize and focus energies to realize their economic ambitions. Some countries mobilized through top-down pressures exerted by the organs of the state. Being small, open, and democratic societies, Sifire relied more on networks to arrive at objectives that commanded broad support. The exchange of views and ease of interaction was facilitated by the relatively egalitarian nature of the societies and the social proximity of the elites to the public. Social distances were small and permitted

---

[13]Inkpen and Tsang (2005) stress the contribution of social capital to networking but also point out that networking exclusivity can interfere with the flow of knowledge from external sources not part of the network. Leamer and Storper (2001) refer to the importance of face-to-face interaction and how information technology seems to encourage such exchanges.

[14]The key message of the network view is that firms are not self-sufficient, and cooperation that leverages external resources can enhance a firm's competitiveness. Harryson (2006, 93) states that a "network perspective aims at understanding the totality of relationships and how they jointly accomplish the result.... Organizations and large corporations can be regarded and analyzed as integrated networks of complex communication linkages, interdependent actors and activities, and cross-organizational/corporate flows of resources."

wide networking and engagement on major national issues. Networking proved effective when countries needed to extricate themselves from crises; it was also effective in building and maintaining economic momentum—at least for two decades.

Absorbing technology to bring industry closer to international best practice and innovating to heighten competitiveness have become a multidisciplinary enterprise for the majority of industrial products. Whether they are part of the food sector, the machine-building sector, or telecommunications, firms and industries must marshal a variety of skills to solve problems and arrive at profitable innovations. Increasingly, firms, or project teams more generally, must seek collaborative arrangements with other parties and tap a number of sources of expertise. Preexisting or newly formed knowledge networks are a means of finding solutions. Such networks are more easily mobilized if the social environment favors relationships based on trust.[15]

Sifire countries proved resourceful in creating intraurban and intracountry networks, and they were also successful in linking with international networks. Globalization enlarged the scope for such networking, and information technology has made it immensely easier to be connected. For smaller economies determined to develop rapidly and catch up with the technological leaders, international networking quickly became essential, whether it was in securing trade opportunities and access to foreign markets, attracting FDI, discovering profitable overseas investment possibilities, or enhancing technology flows and building knowledge capital (OECD 2007). For Ireland and Singapore, the Irish and Chinese diasporas provided the basis for business networks that facilitated trade by providing contacts and serving as intermediaries to attract FDI.[16] A common lingua franca—English, spoken in all three countries—made it easier to participate in global networks and, specifically, to network with U.S. companies and institutions. Knowledge networking, crucial for speeding up technology acquisition

---

[15]Shapin (2010) observes that science in particular relies on trust because only a small fraction of society can command the expertise to adequately comprehend the world of science. So the vast majority depends not on firsthand knowledge but on social categories and institutions that designate certain knowledge producers as trustworthy. The leaking of e-mails from the University of East Anglia's Climate Research Unit was so damaging because it called into question the trust that was reposed in the scientific establishment studying the still deeply contested evidence on the extent and trends of anthropogenic global warming. The leaks, dubbed "Climategate," destroyed the waverers' trust in the integrity of scientists and confirmed the beliefs of those who have always thought that global warming was a myth.

[16]An estimated 70 million to 80 million people worldwide can claim Irish ancestry, with the majority living in the United Kingdom followed by the United States. See Rauch and Trindade (2002) on the role of Asian business intermediaries.

and nurturing innovation, was aided by investments in education—in particular tertiary-level science, technology, engineering, and mathematics, as discussed in chapters 3 and 5—that were sufficient to absorb new technologies and manufacturing practices at a rapid pace. The accumulation of high-quality knowledge capital in the Sifire group during the 1990s and incentives to local institutions and firms to embark on research hooked these countries to globe-spanning knowledge networks that drive brain and idea circulation and make possible collaborative problem solving. Sifire countries were able to engage fruitfully with these networks in an amazingly short time, partly because knowledge and technology were widely accepted as the stepping-stones to prosperity and partly because all three countries started from a higher threshold than the average low-income country. Finland and Ireland lagged the advanced Western European countries in the 1980s, and Singapore was some distance from Europe and Japan. But all three had built a human capital base by investing efficiently in education from the 1960s. Sifire's competitors were also investing, but these three countries squeezed the extra mileage and showed themselves capable of speeds that eluded others.

The critical elements of networking for the purposes of technological catchup—acquiring the tacit knowledge so vital for technological upgrading and efficiency and achieving commercial success in domestic and export markets—are hard to distill into a recipe. It is one thing to render networks mathematically,[17] yet quite another to explain in detail how social networks can be assembled. Networks benefit from social capital and trust; they rarely form involuntarily but call for initiative, interaction, and exchange. They do respond to policy initiatives and incentives, and governments can take the lead in setting up networks, as the governments of Sifire did at various levels to promote manufacturing and technological capabilities. Small countries are under greater pressure to exploit the power of networks to arrive at a more complex and advanced economic structure or to risk being left behind in a more integrated world.

---

[17]Graph theory provides a tool to analyze networks.

References

Adams, James D. 2004. "Scientific Teams and Institution Collaborations: Evidence from U.S. Universities, 1981–1999." NBER Working Paper 10640, National Bureau of Economic Research, Cambridge, MA.

Chan, Chin Bock, ed. 2011. *Heart Work*. 2 vols. Singapore: Straits Times Press.

Dahlman, Carl J., Jorma Routti, and Pekka Ylä-Anttila. 2006. *Finland as a Knowledge Economy: Elements of Success and Lessons Learned*. Washington, DC: World Bank.

Dixit, Avinash. 2007a. "Evaluating Recipes for Development Success." *World Bank Research Observer* 22 (2): 131–57.

———. 2007b. "Governance Institutions and Development." Princeton University, Princeton, NJ. http://www.rbi.org.in/Upload/Publications/PDFs/78261.pdf.

———. 2009. "Governance Institutions and Economic Activity." *American Economic Review* 99 (1): 5–24.

Economist. 2004. "The Luck of the Irish: A Survey of Ireland." *Economist*, October 14.

Glaeser, Edward L., and Matthew G. Resseger. 2009. "The Complementarity between Cities and Skills." NBER Working Paper 15103, National Bureau of Economic Research, Cambridge, MA.

Harryson, Sigvald J. 2006. "The Japanese Know-Who Based Model of Innovation Management." In *Management of Technology and Innovation in Japan*, ed. Cornelius Herstatt, Christoph Stockstrom, Hugo Tschirky, and Akio Nagahira, 87–111. Berlin: Springer-Verlag.

Honohan, Patrick, and Brendan Walsh. 2002. "Catching Up with the Leaders: The Irish Hare." *Brookings Papers on Economic Activity* 33 (1): 1–78.

Huff, Toby E. 1993. *The Rise of Early Modern Science: Islam, China, and the West*. Cambridge, U.K.: Cambridge University Press.

Hung, Shih-Chang. 2000. "Social Construction of Industrial Advantage." *Technovation* 20 (4): 197–203.

IDA (Industrial Development Agency). 2009. "Annual Report 2009." IDA, Dublin. http://www.idaireland.com/news-media/publications/annual-reports/accesible-versions/2009/finance.html.

Inkpen, Andrew C., and Eric W. K. Tsang. 2005. "Networks, Social Capital, and Learning." *Academy of Management Review* 30 (1): 146–65.

Kanbur, Ravi. 2009. "The Crisis, Economic Development Thinking, and Protecting the Poor." Presentation to the World Bank Executive Board, Washington, DC, World Bank. http://kanbur.dyson.cornell.edu/papers/WorldBankBoardPresentation7July09.pdf.

Kumar, Sree, and Sharon Siddique. 2010. "The Singaporean Success Story: Public-Private Alliance for Investment Attraction, Innovation, and Export Development." Serie Comercio Internacional 99, Division of International Trade and Integration, Economic Commission for Latin America and the Caribbean, Santiago.

Leamer, Edward E., and Michael Storper. 2001. "The Economic Geography of the Internet Age." NBER Working Paper 8450, National Bureau of Economic Research, Cambridge, MA.

Lerner, Josh. 2009. "Jamaica vs. Singapore." *American*, November 19.

Meisenzahl, Ralf, and Joel Mokyr. 2011. "The Rate and Direction of Invention in the British Industrial Revolution: Incentives and Institutions." NBER Working Paper 16993, National Bureau of Economic Research, Cambridge, MA.

Ministry of Education and Ministry of Employment and the Economy. 2009. *Evaluation of the Finnish National Innovation System: Full Report.* Helsinki: Taloustieto Oy. http://www.evaluation.fi.

Mokyr, Joel. 2002. *The Gifts of Athena: Historical Origins of the Knowledge Economy.* Princeton, NJ: Princeton University Press.

OECD (Organisation for Economic Co-operation and Development). 2007. "Innovation and Growth: Rationale for an Innovation Strategy." OECD, Paris.

O'Riain, Seán. 2000. "The Flexible Developmental State: Globalization, Information Technology, and the 'Celtic Tiger.'" *Politics and Society* 28 (2): 157–93.

Putnam, Robert D. 2007. "E Pluribus Unum: Diversity and Community in the Twenty-First Century—The 2006 Johan Skytte Prize Lecture." *Scandinavian Political Studies* 30 (2): 137–74.

Rauch, James E., and Vitor Trindade. 2002. "Ethnic Chinese Networks in International Trade." *Review of Economics and Statistics* 84 (1): 116–30.

Rodrik, Dani, Arvind Subramanian, and Francesco Trebbi. 2002. "Institutions Rule: The Primacy of Institutions over Geography and Integration in Economic Development." NBER Working Paper 9305, National Bureau of Economic Research, Cambridge, MA.

Shapin, Steven. 1996. *The Scientific Revolution.* Chicago: University of Chicago Press.

———. 2010. *Never Pure: Historical Studies of Science as If It Was Produced by People with Bodies, Situated in Time, Space, Culture, and Society, and Struggling for Credibility and Authority.* Baltimore, MD: Johns Hopkins University Press.

Srinivas, Smita, and Kimmo Viljamaa. 2003. "BioTurku: 'Newly' Innovative? The Rise of Bio-pharmaceuticals and the Biotech Concentration in Southwest Finland." MIT IPC Working Paper 03-006, Industrial Performance Center, Massachusetts Institute of Technology, Cambridge, MA.

UNIDO (United Nations Industrial Development Organization). 2005. *Industrial Development Report 2005: Capability Building for Catching-Up—Historical, Empirical, and Policy Dimensions.* Vienna, Austria: UNIDO.

5

Delivering Quality Education

Human capital contributes to growth, but educating more people does not cause growth or an increase in jobs, as many countries with legions of unemployed educated youths are discovering.[1] If there is demand and companies perceive opportunities for profiting, then the availability of educated workers makes it easier for firms to expand production and encourages them to invest in additional capacity. Thus, in the presence of demand—actual or latent—augmenting the supply of human capital has the potential to support a virtuous spiral of growth. Globalization set the stage for demand growth, which some countries were quick to exploit, with Singapore, Finland, and Ireland (Sifire) being among the enterprising few. Their efforts at penetrating international markets and servicing domestic demand were buttressed by favorable labor market developments.

If all that the Sifire countries did was provide universal primary education and increase the percentage of students completing secondary schools, their success would be harder to account for.[2] The average number of years of schooling

---

[1] Even advanced countries with comparative advantage in knowledge-intensive activities are having a difficult time generating well-paid jobs for people with doctoral qualifications in science and technology fields (Cyranoski and others 2011).

[2] As Hanushek and Woessmann (2009, 1) observe, "Schooling and human capital investments have been a central focus of development policy, but doubts have arisen as disappointments with results grow. Nowhere is this more apparent than in the case of growth policy, where schooling investments have not appeared to return the economic outcomes promised by growth models."

of a country's workforce has limited explanatory power in growth regressions. Sifire countries differ from the other low- and middle-income countries that expanded school enrollment in several respects. They were able to raise the average quality of the education imparted to ensure that a high percentage of secondary- and tertiary-level students had good science, technology, engineering, and mathematics (STEM) skills and graduated with science and engineering degrees[3] and to see that a significant percentage of students—as high as 40 percent a year—received vocational training of relevance to industrial employers. Sifire further ensured that the average student performed at a higher level than students in most other countries. The Sifire countries were able to pull off this remarkable feat in a relatively short span of time and at costs comparable to or lower than those incurred by other Organisation for Economic Co-operation and Development (OECD) countries.

One of the most intriguing findings reported in the growth literature is the contribution of education quality measured by international test scores of secondary school students in math, science, and reading. Hanushek and Woessmann (2007) find that the excellence of human capital is a potent explanatory variable in growth equations and an intuitively plausible finding.[4] This finding is especially relevant for middle-income countries aiming at higher value-adding segments of markets for products or services and competing on quality, technology, and innovation.[5] All countries gain when they improve the quality of education, but the boost to middle-income countries is arguably greater because they are the ones moving into more skill-intensive activities and are closer to the technology frontier. The broad base and average quality of skills is one major determinant of economic performance. But Sifire derived additional mileage from the number and quality of the top-performing students—those with Programme for International Student Assessment (PISA) test scores above 625. The importance of the numbers of students in the upper tail of the student achievement distribution is brought out by the comparative analysis by Pritchett and Viarengo (2010).[6] It is supported by the findings of Hanushek and Woessmann (2009, 25),

---

[3]In 2005, 23 percent of OECD students graduated with science and engineering degrees compared with 16 percent in the United States (Oxford Analytica 2006).

[4]Using additional time series data and test score results, Appleton, Atherton, and Bleaney (2010) reaffirm the relationship observed by Hanushek and Woessmann (2007), although their estimated coefficients are smaller.

[5]Dalia Marin (2008, 5) labels human capital as the "new stakeholder" in a firm that views talent, not plant and machinery, as the critical asset.

[6]The quality of education in Finland added 0.5 percentage points to annual productivity growth during 1990–2003. See Honkapohja and others (2009).

whose "estimates suggest that developing basic skills and highly talented people reinforce each other."[7]

The Power of Quality Education

How did the Sifire countries achieve the quality outcomes in education that eluded most of their competitors? Before tackling this question, note that Finland and Singapore have attained results superior to those of Ireland, as is clear from the data in chapter 3. The data reflect the overall focus of the policy and strategic commitment to upgrading the workforce. Also note that the Sifire countries have centralized school systems with curricula and standards established by education ministries. In Ireland, the Roman Catholic Church also has a hand in designing instruction on religion at the primary level. The state pays for education from primary through university levels in Finland and Ireland,[8] with the private sector playing a minimal role in Ireland. Singapore provides largely free primary and secondary schooling in state schools.[9] Tertiary-level education is subsidized by the state. Private primary and secondary schools coexist with public schools in Ireland and Singapore.

The exhaustive research on schooling has helped to narrow the factors responsible for student performance, but inevitably opinions remain divided.[10] The experience of Sifire points to the importance of six factors. First, raising and sustaining student performance at high levels are inseparable from nonschool factors such as family circumstances, the value a society attaches to education, and the

---

[7]Hanushek and Woessmann (2009, 25) further observe that "achieving basic literacy for all may well be a precondition for identifying those who can reach 'rocket scientist' status." Because many countries are well on their way to realizing the objective of basic literacy, there is now an urgent need to fatten the upper tail of the quality distribution, which is frequently underpopulated. Mexico, the country singled out by Pritchett and Viarengo (2010), is severely deficient in this regard. Only 0.29 percent of Mexican students who took the PISA test had scores in excess of 625 (the advanced benchmark), compared with 18.5 percent of students from the Republic of Korea and 6.5 percent of students from the United States. In other words, Mexico produces fewer than 6,000 students a year who fall in the advanced category. Even the Slovak Republic, a much smaller country, has a larger number of high-performing students.

[8]Only students from the European Union qualify for free education. Students in Ireland must pay a registration fee.

[9]There is a small copayment required at the secondary level.

[10]Hanushek (2008) discounts factors such as school facilities and class size and singles out teacher quality, although identifying the determinants of teacher performance is difficult. Heckman, Carneiro, and Cunha (2004) also downplay school resources and school quality.

conviction that excellence is necessary for progress toward a better, innovative, and more prosperous society.[11] It is not only small countries that are likely to seek high standards—there are plenty of examples to the contrary. However, smallness and ethnic homogeneity can lead to the coalescing of cultural norms that induce nations to try harder to progress in a competitive world.[12]

Second, quality needs to be pervasive, extending from the primary all the way to vocational and tertiary levels. Heckman and his coworkers (Cunha and Heckman 2007) have found that foundational capabilities instilled by the earlier stages of schooling, when children are three to six years of age, exert a strong influence on later cognitive as well as noncognitive development.[13] Each level of schooling provides the needed preparation for good performance at the next stage. Obtaining a high average scholastic performance for the student body demands that virtually all primary and middle school students be equipped with a threshold level of knowledge and skills and that every effort be made to shrink the left tail of the performance distribution (Hanushek 2010; OECD 2010). Those lacking in scholastic aptitude need opportunities to acquire other useful skills by taking a vocational route.

Third, student performance and the pursuit of excellence must continually be reinforced by family and social environments.[14] The importance of parental input scarcely needs emphasizing. Better-educated parents and intact families are more effective in inculcating values that encourage learning and good study habits (Cunha and Heckman 2007).[15] The surveys conducted as a part of Trends in International Mathematics and Science Study (TIMSS) show that student attitudes and motivation

---

[11]OECD (2010) refers to the importance Confucian culture attaches to education but also notes that countries such as Canada and Finland are equally committed. Education quality also promotes innovation (Varsakelis 2006).

[12]Fernandez (2010) provides a compelling survey of the evidence pointing to the influence of culture on performance.

[13]Lynn and Vanhanen (2006) present evidence showing how a country's IQ scores are correlated with per capita income and also with overall economic performance. Their findings suggest that efforts to raise IQ levels of young children, with the help of a better home environment, nutrition, and early childhood education can have a handsome payoff. Cunha and Heckman (2007, 3–4) point to "critical and sensitive periods in the development of a child.... IQ scores become stable at the age of 10. And the later remediation is given to a disadvantaged child, the less effective it is."

[14]Gould, Lavy, and Paserman (2009) describe how immigrant children from the Republic of Yemen, placed in good socioeconomic environments in Israel, did better in school, married at a later age, and integrated better with the rest of society. The academic drift of students in the United States, as noted by Arum and Roksa (2011), may in part reflect a weakening of the learning environment in universities and in society more generally.

[15]The higher the parental education level, the greater are the chances that one or both parents will keep a watchful eye on a child's performance—and that of the school—and communicate with teachers about lapses or problems. Parental interest is as important a check on schools as is monitoring by public agencies.

bear on their test results. This motivation derives from social mores stressing achievement as well as from the expectations instilled by the family (Yusuf and others 2003).[16] In societies where income and wealth are more equally distributed, social norms enjoy wider acceptance and there is greater uniformity of family circumstances and family values. More egalitarian societies also find it easier to reorient themselves in response to crises—or fresh opportunities—and to search for and adopt new social bearings in response to changes in the economic or political environment.

Not very long ago, Confucian cultures were derided as dysfunctional and conservative and as lacking the entrepreneurial and progressive attitudes emblematic of modern capitalist societies.[17] First Japan, followed by the Republic of Korea and Taiwan, China, and most recently China, falsified these views. No society is too conservative to avoid change at any cost. The East Asian economies demonstrated that the more egalitarian and culturally homogeneous societies are quicker to shift tracks and to mobilize in support of new norms. Economically stagnant East Asian societies were transformed into tigers overnight when new leadership began making the case for a different strategy and reordering the rules of the game, complete with incentives and penalties.

Much of the research and experimentation on how to provide quality education has been done in the United States, but the task of winnowing through the welter of conflicting findings to construct a coherent system on a nationwide scale has been left to other countries (see Hanushek 2010; Hanushek and Rivkin 2006). A fourth factor that influences student performance is teacher qualifications. Sifire settled early on good teachers as the vehicles for imparting the education and skills needed by a modern-day workforce.[18] By setting high standards and expectations

---

[16]Richard Posner (2011) has stressed the importance of education to instill civic values in a developing country's youths—values that include honesty, respect for knowledge, tolerance, and—of perhaps greatest importance—loyalty to national institutions.

[17]Max Weber was the foremost exponent of this view, which he expounded in two famous books: *The Religion of China* (Weber 1951) and *The Protestant Ethic and the Spirit of Capitalism* (Weber 1958).

[18]Recent research has confirmed the wisdom of the policy that singled out teaching capabilities as the key objective. Hanushek (2010, iii) calculates that in the United States the marginal gains of US$400,000 in the present value of earning would accrue to a student from a "teacher one standard deviation above the mean effectiveness." Were the United States to replace the least effective 8 percent of teachers with average teachers, the country could bring student achievement close to that of Finland. "The estimates of growth impacts of bringing U.S. students up to Finland imply astounding improvements in the well-being of U.S. citizens. The present value of future increments to GDP in the U.S. would amount to $112 trillion" (Hanushek, 2010, 23). But Hanushek's review of the literature also draws attention to how difficult it is to identify the measures that will make teachers deliver results (Hanushek 2010; Hanushek and Rivkin 2006; see also Goldhaber 2002). Another article (*Economist* 2011, 25) emphasizes the role of teachers and states, "Better teachers take much longer to form. They should be made the priority."

for teachers and by steadfastly adhering to these standards, Sifire stiffened and rein-forced the social ethic underpinning the quest for excellence. There is no uniformity in the approaches to selecting and training teachers. However, all countries have var-iously used similar criteria. Teacher qualifications are pitched high—generally grad-uate-level degrees[19]—and the selection criteria are demanding, especially in Finland and Singapore.[20] Teacher education and frequent in-service training to upgrade skills are seen as helpful for maintaining standards.[21]

A fifth factor is pay and prestige. To attract and retain some of the most talented in the teaching profession, Sifire offered competitive salaries and job security and used effective personnel management practices.[22] Teaching in the Sifire countries has also been treated as a high-status occupation, with teachers enjoying considerable prestige in society (OECD 2010). That standing partially compensates for incomes that might be somewhat less than the highest offered by the market. Research reported by McKinsey Global Institute (2010) indicates that the best-performing education systems have drawn a proportionately larger number of teachers from the most able university graduates—those in the upper right-hand tail of the distribution. Finland, Ireland, and Singapore are among the countries that have filled the ranks of the teaching profession with some of the ablest graduates. Teacher performance appears to have been buttressed by rewards and social recognition (see Sahlberg 2011).

The sixth factor calls for a measure of teacher autonomy in fine-tuning the cur-riculum and pedagogical techniques and in evaluating students. In this respect, Finland has given teachers the greatest latitude, and Finnish teachers devote less time to classroom instruction than teachers in the two other countries. Teachers in Singapore also enjoy substantial autonomy.[23] Thus, nationally uniform curricula

---

[19]All Finnish teachers must have at least a master's degree. Hanushek (2010) notes, how-ever, that teachers with higher qualifications are not, on average, more effective than those with fewer degrees.

[20]Singapore's college administrators identify individuals they would like to draw into the teaching profession and offer them a variety of incentives to take up teaching. Singapore also offers teachers highly competitive salaries.

[21]However, Hanushek (2010, 5) cites research showing that "even very intensive professional development to help teachers become more effective after they are already in the classroom has shown little impact on student achievement."

[22]Hanushek (2010) observes that the attraction of the teaching profession in Finland could not be because of high salaries. Research reported by Loeb, Kalogrides, and Béteille (2011) shows that successful schools selectively seek better teachers from the available pool and exert more effort at retaining them. Moreover, there is a virtuous cycle at work: a school's performance in the past motivates improvement in the performance of teachers in subsequent periods.

[23]An OECD (2010) report draws attention to the limited amount of time devoted to classroom lectures in the best-performing systems. Rather, teachers engage in group discussions and make every effort to draw out students and get to know their strengths and limitations so as to better assist them.

and standards are combined with a freer hand at the school level, a practice that permits microlevel adjustments based on differences in teacher capabilities and the characteristics of students (on Finland, see Sahlberg 2011). In addition, this approach leaves room for experimentation. Careful selection of school principals in Singapore, recognition of merit, and rotation of principals among schools are part and parcel of the effort to raise the average quality of schools.[24]

In one important area of pedagogical technique, Finland and Singapore have diverged. Singapore, in keeping with practice across East Asia, has favored the rigorous drilling of students, a lengthy school year, and homework. Finland adopted a different tack: a short school year, little homework, fewer hours of instruction by the teacher,[25] and greater independence for the student to pursue studies. Both approaches have produced outstanding scholastic outcomes in their respective social environments. Ireland is in between. Singapore worries that a highly structured approach that includes drilling risks draining students of creativity and analytic skills. However, Finland's concern is that in the current milieu, with its numerous distractions, students may slacken and turn away from the hard sciences, a trend visible throughout the world and notably in Ireland. The debate on how to combine performance and knowledge accumulation with creativity continues.

Vocational Training

In addition to raising the quality of general education, many industrializing countries have struggled to make a success of vocational training. Such training is the appropriate path for students whose aptitude is for the practical and for working with their hands. Industry values not just good basic education but also practical skills suited for the majority of jobs. Unfortunately, cultural predispositions that shape parental preferences assign a lower ranking to vocational qualifications, and vocational school graduates often see themselves as a cut below those who have received general schooling. Moreover, few countries have been able to develop an effective system of vocational schools because such training is costly and needs to mesh with emerging market demands. The Sifire group is conspicuous in having crafted a system of vocational schools and polytechnics catering to between

---

[24]Evidence showing that salaries motivate teachers and are reflected in the performance of students can be found in Figlio and Kenny (2006). On the issue of autonomy, it should be noted that Finland is moving away from tight central regulation and financing of the tertiary education system and is modifying university governance as well as financing structures (Aarrevaara, Dobson, and Elander 2009).

[25]A detailed analysis of the PISA 2006 data from 50 countries by Lavy (2010) revealed that the time devoted to instruction by teachers has a positive and significant effect on the test scores of 15-year-olds. Hence, the Finnish results might not carry over to other countries and cultures.

one-third and one-half of the post–primary school student body with the objective of equipping graduates with marketable skills.[26]

As with general schooling, the vocational training outcomes have varied among the three countries, but they share four attributes. First, the quality of the instructors sets the tone. The ability to recruit better and experienced teachers is a hallmark of quality.

Second, vocational schools need to be well furnished with adequate, up-to-date equipment so that students are trained on machines and software reasonably similar to the equipment they would encounter on the job. The cost of equipment and facilities makes vocational education more expensive than general education. Thus, sufficient financing from public and private sources is key to a viable system.

Third, financing vocational training and structuring the system to deliver the mix of skills that could be readily absorbed require close collaboration with potential employers. Ministries of education, in consultation with businesses, must project future demand for skills and, on the basis of employer feedback, correct deficiencies and consolidate strengths of vocational trainees. Such an effort entails information exchange, analysis, and coordination, not to mention continual adjustments to training programs, to deliver market-conforming results. It is the nature of vocational training that employer involvement with and support for the system are crucial. In Sifire, this effort was facilitated by the proactive role assigned to key economic agencies, the smallness of the countries, and the clustering of most businesses in just three or four cities—all of which made for ease of forecasting and responding to emerging market demands.

Fourth, the efforts of governments would have come to naught if they had failed to convince parents and students of the value of vocational qualifications and how these burnished their job prospects. The Sifire governments realized early the necessity of backstopping industrial and growth ambitions with suitable training institutions to minimize the risk of skill shortages and mismatches. In European countries, the value of technical training has long been recognized; hence, government agencies in Finland and Ireland had a much easier time in augmenting and improving the vocational training system. Singapore had to overcome a deep-seated bias against vocational streaming that required the government to launch an intensive and ongoing campaign of persuasion, to build expensive facilities, and to present evidence that the vocational path led to a rewarding career even under conditions of uncertainty and rapid economic change.

---

[26]The longer-term benefits of vocational education for economies and individuals have been questioned by Hanushek, Woessmann, and Zhang (2011), who find that those with primarily vocational training found it harder to adapt later in life to technological changes and new work routines.

Sustaining Consistent Performance

As in every other country, education in the Sifire countries has its history of short-comings and problems—some corrected and others still demanding attention. Quality education that meets the market test with some consistency is difficult to deliver. The risk of sliding backward is omnipresent, as Germany, Japan, the United Kingdom, and the United States are finding. Increasing spending on education is rarely an answer, an inconvenient fact that advanced countries such as the United States have difficulty coming to terms with.[27] Efficient investment is what counts (OECD 2010). Vested interests—especially teachers unions, where they exist—strenuously oppose change, and better test results do not immediately translate into improved economic outcomes. With technological change coming to be viewed as essential for sustaining growth, Sifire and other countries have increasingly attached a special significance to tertiary education and research.

It was becoming apparent in the 1980s that the intensity of skill levels required by manufacturing and many service industries was on an upward trend, but few could predict how steep a trend it might be. Fewer still could anticipate how rapidly information technology would evolve, filter into every crevice of society, and demand new kinds of literacy and skills. Many countries were slow to acknowledge the cues and to prepare their universities for the leap in quality and content of education. The Sifire countries were among those that read the signs accurately, possibly because by the early 1990s, their leading sectors were among the most research and skill intensive.

The first order of business for these countries was to increase the supply of university graduates with the technical skills likely to be in greatest demand and to ensure that their training conformed to the highest international standards.[28] By enhancing supply and raising standards, the Sifire countries reasoned that they would be able to help their firms catapult into the front ranks of international business and persuade leading multinational corporations to relocate their production, their other functions, and eventually their regional headquarters and some of their research and development activities. To a surprising extent, Ireland and Singapore did achieve this objective. A world-class tertiary education sector was singled out as the long-term driver in a world where business people, economists, and scientists identified innovative technologies as the principal means of growth.

---

[27] Among the OECD countries, the United States spends more on secondary education than only two other countries—Austria and Switzerland—and obtains mediocre results. South Africa, also a high spender, has seen its performance deteriorate over the past decade (see *Economist* 2011).

[28] Aghion and Howitt (1998) and Vandenbussche, Aghion, and Meghir (2004) have shown that the payoff to tertiary-level skills and research and development increases the closer a country moves to the technological frontier.

Sifire showed how university systems, modest in size and middling in capabilities and performance, could be scaled up and staffed with talented people in a short time and at a price these countries could afford. If done efficiently, expanding tertiary education need not be a formidable undertaking for a small country that proceeds strategically in manageable steps with the support of key stakeholders, that is willing to supplement a domestic teaching staff with overseas talent, and that is willing to pay market rates. A coordinated effort by government agencies with the backing of municipal bodies, universities, business interests, and property developers yielded prompt results that were soon reflected in the performance of the three countries.

The universities in Sifire first set their sights on meeting actual and projected demand for well-trained graduates. Only after the initial objectives were being realized, did some universities begin pursuing research agendas in specialized fields. The quest for university and industry research links and the commercialization of research findings is an even more recent departure.[29] Whether universities in Sifire will become research powerhouses remains to be seen. Their global rankings do not yet point to burgeoning capabilities, although the Singapore authorities in particular have been signaling their ambitions to make Singapore a research hub in biotechnology. Undeniable are the staggering achievements telescoped into two decades that have created highly effective university sectors with a strong focus on STEM skills, which are among the most difficult and costly to inculcate.

Starting Almost from Scratch: What It Takes

In this context, three additional points deserve attention. First, none of the countries started with a long-standing academic tradition. Finland and Ireland had small university sectors in the 1960s, and none of the universities were highly ranked. Hence, the subsequent growth of tertiary education was on the narrowest of foundations. Second, the three countries lie on the periphery of regional economic systems and away from the industrial cores of East Asia and Europe. Yet their location did not prevent a coalescence of talent once the tempo of economic activity began accelerating. The Sifire countries were able to groom local talent, retain most of the highly trained workers, and—in Ireland and Singapore—engineer a brain gain from abroad. Both of these factors are heartening, but they do suggest that growing the tertiary sector is predicated on accelerating industrial activity led by export-oriented high-tech activities with sound long-term prospects. Absent a deepening and dynamic industrial base and the buzz associated with high-tech activities that are demonstrating international competitiveness, it is

---

[29]Earlier stages of development involved combining capital with less well-educated workers. Once the focus shifted to technological innovation, it became necessary to increase the supply of higher-level skills.

difficult to envision the emergence of world-class tertiary-level institutions, sources of financing and the demand for skills, and a steady concentration of talent. Primary and secondary schooling, combined with other ingredients, must initiate faster growth before a country can substantially augment tertiary-level skills and their quality and create the employment opportunities.

The final observation is about the urban dimension of tertiary-level education and research institutions. World-class universities flourish in the principal cities. It can hardly be otherwise, especially in small countries. Establishing a major university would be difficult in cities with a population below a threshold of about 500,000 to 700,000.[30] The better-known Finnish universities are in Helsinki, Turku, and Oulu.[31] Irish universities of note are in Dublin, Galway, and Cork. Most of the jobs for university graduates are in cities that host clusters of industrial activity.[32] The earlier point about industrial quickening preceding tertiary sector expansion and upgrading can be given an urban twist. The better institutions are in one of the main cities because the jobs, resources, new starts, and excitement are in those places, and the social and professional networks are more numerous, more dense, and more rewarding. If there is an urban agglomeration strand to the Sifire story, it is a very minor one. Aside from Singapore, the cities of Finland and Ireland are midsized or small. The spectacular growth was localized, inevitably, and induced a concentration of talent that further perpetuated the narrow geographic focus of development.

Progress on the institutional front enabled Sifire to push ahead with accumulating human capital, the driver of endogenous growth. The three countries differed in the degree to which they could invest in the education system, but by focusing on the workforce, they all greatly improved the economic odds in their favor. Research on the contribution of human capital to growth has yielded equivocal results; however, the progressive refinement of hypotheses and of their testing is providing clarification (see Aghion and others 2009). It is also helping to align

---

[30]This is by no means an iron rule. Cambridge University, a research university ranked second in the world, has flourished in a city with a population of less than 120,000 (250,000 if the periurban area is included). Oxford University thrives in a city of 130,000. Many of the famous university towns in Europe are as small, if not smaller. However, most are adjacent to larger cities and benefit from their agglomeration economies. University scale remains a consideration, and Finland is taking steps to merge its 20 universities into fewer and more viable units (Aarrevaara, Dobson, and Elander 2009).

[31]The University of Turku is Finland's second-largest university, and the Turku University of Applied Sciences is the nation's largest polytechnic. Oulu's capabilities in electronics and information technology were built by the University of Oulu (Chakrabarti and Rice 2003).

[32]Larger cities also stand a better chance of retaining students who come from elsewhere to study in their universities.

the role of human capital with the workings of endogenous growth models (see Lucas 1990; Romer 1989; Warsh 2006).

References

Aarrevaara, Timo, Ian R. Dobson, and Camilla Elander. 2009. "Brave New World: Higher Education Reform in Finland." *Higher Education Management and Policy* 21 (2): 87–104.

Aghion, Philippe, Leah Boustan, Caroline Hoxby, and Jerome Vandenbussche. 2009. "The Causal Impact of Education on Economic Growth: Evidence from U.S." Brookings Papers on Economic Activity, Brookings Institution, Washington, DC.

Aghion, Philippe, and Peter Howitt. 1998. *Endogenous Growth Theory*. Cambridge, MA: MIT Press.

Appleton, Simon, Paul Atherton, and Michael Bleaney. 2010. "International School Test Scores and Economic Growth." CREDIT Research Paper 08/04, Centre for Research in Economic Development and International Trade, University of Nottingham, Nottingham, U.K.

Arum, Richard, and Josipa Roksa. 2011. *Academically Adrift: Limited Learning on College Campuses*. Chicago: University of Chicago Press.

Chakrabarti, Alok K., and Mark Rice. 2003. "Changing Roles of Universities in Developing Entrepreneurial Regions: The Case of Finland and the U.S." MIT-IPC Working Paper 03-003, Industrial Performance Center, Massachusetts Institute of Technology, Cambridge, MA.

Cunha, Flavio, and James J. Heckman. 2007. "The Technology of Skill Formation." NBER Working Paper 12840, National Bureau of Economic Research, Cambridge, MA. http://www.nber.org/papers/w12840.pdf.

Cyranoski, David, Natasha Gilbert, Heidi Ledford, Anjali Nayer, and Mohammed Yahia. 2011. "Education: The PhD Factory." *Nature* 472: 276–79. http://www.nature.com/news/2011/110420/full/472276a.html.

Economist. 2011. "Reforming Education: The Great Schools Revolution." *Economist*, September 17.

Fernandez, Raquel. 2010. "Does Culture Matter?" CEPR Discussion Paper DP7965, Centre for Economic Policy Research, London.

Figlio, David N., and Lawrence Kenny. 2006. "Individual Teacher Incentives and Student Performance." NBER Working Paper 12627, National Bureau of Economic Research, Cambridge, MA.

Goldhaber, Dan. 2002. "The Mystery of Good Teaching." *Education Next* 2 (1): 50–55.

Gould, Eric D., Victor Lavy, and M. Daniele Paserman. 2009. "Sixty Years after the Magic Carpet Ride: The Long-Run Effect of the Early Childhood Environment on Social and Economic Outcomes." NBER Working Paper 14884, National Bureau of Economic Research, Cambridge, MA.

Hanushek, Eric A. 2008. "Education Production Functions." In *The New Palgrave Dictionary of Economics*, 2nd ed., ed. Steven N. Durlauf and Lawrence E. Blume. Basingstoke, U.K.: Palgrave Macmillan.

———. 2010. "The Economic Value of Higher Teacher Quality." CALDER Working Paper 56, National Center for Analysis of Longitudinal Data in Education Research, Urban

Institute, Washington, DC. http://www.urban.org/uploadedpdf/1001507-Higher-Teacher-Quality.pdf.

Hanushek, Eric A., and Steven Rivkin. 2006. "School Quality and the Black-White Achievement Gap." NBER Working Paper 12651, National Bureau of Economic Research, Cambridge, MA.

Hanushek, Eric A., and Ludger Woessmann. 2007. "The Role of Education Policy for Economic Growth." Policy Research Working Paper 4122, World Bank, Washington, DC.

———. 2009. "Do Better Schools Lead to More Growth? Cognitive Skills, Economic Outcomes, and Causation." NBER Working Paper 14633, National Bureau of Economic Research, Cambridge, MA.

Hanushek, Eric A., Ludger Woessmann, and Lei Zhang. 2011. "General Education, Vocational Education, and Labor-Market Outcomes over the Life-Cycle." NBER Working Paper 17504, National Bureau of Economic Research, Cambridge, MA.

Heckman, James J., Pedro Carneiro, and Flavio Cunha. 2004. "The Technology of Skill Formation." 2004 Meeting Paper 681, Society for Economic Dynamics, Federal Reserve Bank of St. Louis, St. Louis, MO.

Honkapohja, Seppo, Erkki A. Koskela, Willi Leibfritz, and Roope Uusitalo. 2009. *Economic Prosperity Recaptured: The Finnish Path from Crisis to Rapid Growth*. Cambridge MA: MIT Press.

Lavy, Victor. 2010. "Do Differences in School's Instruction Time Explain International Achievement Gaps in Math, Science, and Reading? Evidence from Developed and Developing Countries." NBER Working Paper 16227, National Bureau of Economic Research, Cambridge, MA.

Loeb, Susanna, Demetra Kalogrides, and Tara Béteille. 2011. "Effective Schools: Demonstrating Recruitment, Assignment, Development, and Retention of Effective Teachers." NBER Working Paper 17177, National Bureau of Economic Research, Cambridge, MA.

Lucas, Robert. 1990. "On the Mechanics of Economic Development." *Journal of Monetary Economics* 22(1): 3–42.

Lynn, Richard, and Tatu Vanhanen. 2006. *IQ and Global Inequality*. Whitefish, MT: Washington Summit.

Marin, Dalia. 2008. "The New Corporation in Europe." Policy Brief 2008/07, Bruegel, Brussels.

McKinsey & Company. 2010. "Closing the Talent Gap: Attracting and Retaining Top Third Graduates to a Career in Teaching." McKinsey & Company, Washington, DC.

OECD (Organisation for Economic Co-operation and Development). 2010. *Strong Performers and Successful Reformers of Education: Lessons from PISA for the United States*. Paris: OECD.

Oxford Analytica. 2006. "R&D Moves to Developing Countries." Oxford Analytica, September 25.

Posner, Richard. 2011. "What Is a College Degree Really Worth?" *Becker-Posner Blog*, March 14. http://www.becker-posner-blog.com/2011/03/what-is-a-college-degree-really-worthposner.html.

Pritchett, Lant, and Martina Viarengo. 2010. "Producing Superstars for the Economic Mundial: The Team in the Tail." VoxEU.org, August 20. http://voxeu.org/index.php?q= node/5422.

Romer, Paul M. 1989. "Human Capital and Growth: Theory and Evidence." NBER Working Paper 3173, National Bureau of Economic Research, Cambridge, MA.

Sahlberg, Pasi. 2011. *Finnish Lessons.* New York: Teachers College Press.

Vandenbussche, Jérôme, Philippe Aghion, and Costas Meghir. 2004. "Growth, Distance to the Frontier, and the Composition of Human Capital." Department of Economics, Harvard University, Cambridge, MA.

Varsakelis, Nikos C. 2006. "Education, Political Institutions, and Innovative Activity: A Cross-Country Empirical Investigation." *Research Policy* 35 (7): 1083–90.

Warsh, David. 2006. *Knowledge and the Wealth of Nations: A Story of Economic Discovery.* New York: W.W. Norton.

Weber, Max. 1951. *The Religion of China: Confucianism and Taoism.* New York: Free Press.

———. 1958. *The Protestant Ethic and the Spirit of Capitalism.* New York: Charles Scribner's Sons.

Yusuf, Shahid, M. Anjum Altaf, Barry Eichengreen, Sudarshan Gooptu, Kaoru Nabeshima, Charles Kenny, Dwight H. Perkins, and Marc Shotten. 2003. *Innovative East Asia: The Future of Growth.* Washington, DC: World Bank.

6

The Message from Sifire

An observer in the mid 1980s could not have imagined how much economic ground Singapore, Finland, and Ireland (Sifire) could cover by 2005. The three economies looked frail and their longer-term prospects seemed uncertain. Ten years later they were flying high, and over the course of another decade, they had gained admission to the club of high-income economies. A mere three years after that, in 2008, Ireland was in the grip of a severe crisis that threatened its hard-won prosperity and suspended a question over its economic future. This crisis resulted not from a failure of Ireland's knowledge-based growth model but from a bank credit–fueled, highly speculative real estate bubble[1] and the subsequent socialization of the extraordinary liabilities of private banks by the Irish government (Portes 2011). Although Finland is recovering from the financial crisis of 2008 and 2009, its medium-term growth prospects appear less promising.[2] Its flagship telecommunications company, Nokia, is losing global market share in the face of competition from nimbler rivals, which have been quicker to introduce cost, design, and product innovations—firms such as Apple, HTC, Huawei, RIM,

---

[1] In 2006, at the height of the boom, construction accounted for almost a quarter of Ireland's gross domestic product and employed close to 20 percent of the workforce. Between 1994 and 2006, the cost of an average home in Dublin rose by 500 percent (Lewis 2011). Lewis (2011, 184) claims, "The Irish real estate bubble was different from the American version in many ways: it wasn't disguised, for a start; it did not require a lot of financial engineering beyond the understanding of mere mortals; it also wasn't as cynical . . . in Ireland the big shots went down with the banks."

[2] In 2009, Finland's gross domestic product fell by 7.8 percent because of a 24 percent drop in exports and a 13 percent decline in investment. This downturn was the worst ever experienced by Finland, and the economy has struggled to recover with investment remaining sluggish in 2011 (Oxford Analytica 2010a). See also HelsinginSanomat (2004).

Samsung, and ZTE. Meanwhile, biotech clusters and other traditional industries are unable to provide alternative engines of growth.[3] Only Singapore is in good health, having recovered smartly from the financial crisis of 2008 and 2009 and having averaged a growth rate of 12 percent during 2009 and 2010. But with nonoil exports amounting to 75 percent of gross domestic product (GDP), Singapore is highly vulnerable to trade and currency wars and the retreat of globalization.[4]

The painful events that clouded the last three years of the "noughties" cannot diminish the remarkable economic progress by the three countries against considerable odds. Nor does the postcrisis slowdown detract from the relevance of their experience for ambitious low- and middle-income countries. This final chapter parses a few of the enduring lessons for late starters and the smaller middle-income economies and indicates how these lessons need to be tempered in light of recent shocks and the forces now pressing on the global economy.

The experience of Sifire offers heartening evidence that quite simple recipes that are vigorously implemented can produce dramatic results when a country can take advantage of the winds of globalization to generate demand, acquire technology, and supplement domestic resources of human and physical capital. Sifire's development over approximately two decades (extending from 1985 to 2005) underscores the potency of two sets of ingredients. One set comprises the development institutions that plan and implement economic policies and the public agencies and key private entities that, through their coordination and networking capabilities, agree on and jointly pursue economic objectives. The second set comprises the elements of the learning and innovation system and the means of achieving desired quality standards.

The Sifire countries also illuminate the role of investment by multinational corporations (MNCs). The foreign direct investment (FDI) story is part of the conventional wisdom on development. For late starters or, for that matter, any country, FDI in the productive sectors and in infrastructure can contribute positively to growth through spillovers and links.[5] Sifire demonstrated how a development strategy backed by efficient institutions and attention to the supply of quality talent underpinned the conventional menu of tax incentives and the provision of infrastructure and urban amenities.

---

[3]Nokia's share of the mobile handset market fell to 27 percent in 2011, and its ranking, according to Interbrand, fell to 14 from 8 in the previous year (http://worldwidegadget.blog spot.com/2012/01/2011-global-handset-market-share-nokia.html; http://www.interbrand .com/en/best-global-brands/best-global-brands-2008/best-global-brands-2011.aspx). On the potential of the biotech cluster in Helsinki, see Breznitz and Tahvanainen (2010).

[4]This vulnerability became apparent in 2008, when exports began dipping sharply and the financial crisis tightened its grip, pulling GDP into negative territory in 2009 by 1.3 percent (Oxford Analytica 2008, 2010d).

[5]Irish experience suggests that smaller foreign firms are more likely to partner with local firms (Görg, Hanley, and Strobl 2010).

Pragmatic Governance

Sifire demonstrated that neither size nor geographic peripherality need pose insuperable obstacles as long as the country is politically mobilized in support of a development strategy credibly tailored to its potential capabilities and buttressed by relevant international experience.[6] Sifire also demonstrated tellingly that a sound strategy, good policies, and the capacity to leverage human resources could, with a bit of luck, serve as sufficient conditions for rapid growth. A close reading of the recent history of Finland and Ireland revealed that they are "normal" countries displaying an average degree of social cohesion and discipline. Both are subject to political give-and-take, are susceptible to slippages or outright failures of governance,[7] and are led by parties and leaders who could not be accused of unusual enlightenment or farsightedness. Singapore, tightly managed by the People's Action Party (PAP) since the 1960s,[8] is closer to the model of the efficient, authoritarian development state, but from necessity, Singapore functioned as a highly open economy, albeit with an illiberal democracy.[9] Openness checked the powers of the state and compelled it to win commitment to demanding policies by continuously demonstrating that it delivered the promised economic rewards. In Albert Hirschman's (1970) terms, the citizens of the three countries could easily avail themselves of the exit option and, to varying degrees, could also exercise voice. When the countries began stepping up the pace, they were much like other industrializing nations and far less well endowed with natural resources than many.

Leveraging Global Markets and General-Purpose Technologies

The winds of trade were beginning to blow strongly when the Sifire group began its dash to the top, and flows of FDI and of portfolio capital were also increasing in volume. The first was a source of demand, the second a source of productive investment, and both embodied technology and spillovers. Ireland and Singapore

---

[6]Smallness and peripherality can constrain innovation because of "small world" problems arising from intense connectivity that homogenizes the material available to members and from excessive cohesiveness that leads to sharing common rather than novel information (see Uzzi and Spiro 2005).

[7]These failures are glaring in Ireland's case. See Foster (2008) and Lewis (2011).

[8]Elections in 2011 led to a sharp decline in the popular vote for the PAP and point to dissatisfaction with rising inequality, in-migration, and the mode of government.

[9]*Illiberal democracy* is a term coined by Fareed Zakaria (1997) to describe countries where regular elections are held but power is centralized and political opposition tightly controlled. See Mutalib (2000, 2003) and Rodan (2006) on the practice of democracy in Singapore.

exploited this situation to the full by using foreign capital to promote industrial development and the widening foreign markets to sell products. Finland also benefited from export demand and a smaller volume of FDI.

In the 1980s, trade and capital were joined by a third growth driver—technology—as the electronics, Internet, and biotech industries began spreading their wings. The Sifire countries combined the power of all three sets of policies described in earlier chapters:

• They created lead development and planning agencies and mechanisms for interagency coordination of objectives and of policies as well as mechanisms for consulting stakeholders in the business, financial, real estate, and education sectors. Lead agencies defined ambitious, albeit feasible, objectives. Most important, they helped strengthen the capability to implement policies and produce results. The critical early stage of development in the late 1980s and early 1990s involved accelerating growth using demand generated by exports and investment. This demand and the growth that followed fed savings and enabled Sifire to push human capital development to a higher plane.

• Starting from a solid base of primary and middle school education, Sifire focused on boosting secondary and tertiary education by emphasizing quality and by promoting science, technology, engineering, and mathematics (STEM) and vocational skills. Chapter 5 discussed how quality objectives were realized within a matter of years. The increased supply of trained workers allowed businesses, both local and foreign, to expand capacity. Businesses supported an upgrading of production technology, that enabled Sifire to take the lead in harnessing information and communication technology (ICT), and they helped the countries advance toward technology frontiers in a number of major and rapidly evolving fields. In addition, businesses supported incremental innovation by combining advanced technical skills with vocational ones.[10] The deepening of tertiary education set the stage for spillovers to industry through research, consulting, internships, incubators, and science parks.

• Globalization, a thick shelf of technological possibilities, better governance and stronger implementation capabilities, effective networking, and an increased supply of human talent can contribute to growth. However, rapid growth is inseparable from the high levels of investment that supplement demand from other sources. Such investment is the primary vehicle for transferring technology and closing technology gaps until countries are ready to move to the innovation stage. Singapore, which has had the highest growth rates, also invested the most, combining domestic savings with FDI. Ireland had lower rates of domestic savings and depended more on FDI and transfers from the European Union (EU). Finland, with more modest FDI flows, relied on domestic resources.

---

[10]See the survey relating skills and work organization to innovation by Toner (2011).

Updating the Sifire Experience

The relevance of all these factors for growth in the smaller lower- and middle-income countries remains pertinent. But looking forward, one sees a need to qualify some of the lessons from Sifire and to add a few more that are based on the experiences from elsewhere.

The industrial drivers of growth in Sifire were ICT, biopharmaceutical, and resource-based products. The importance of the traditional industries should not be forgotten and is of particular relevance for lower-income countries. There is plenty of life and demonstrated scalability in these industries. However, capital-intensive productivity, by enhancing technological change, is measurably diminishing the employment generated and is intensifying the skill requirements in both manufacturing and ICT based services (Brynjolfsson and McAfee 2011; Ford 2009). Furthermore, middle-income producers of ICT-based products are finding that once technological gaps in manufacturing have been erased, pushing the technology frontier through innovation is no easy matter. Small countries with narrow skill bases and specializations find it much harder to gain and sustain a technological lead on the strength of home-grown skills and companies. As Nokia has discovered, anticipating and responding to shifts in the global telecommunication market can be challenging for a company that is not firmly tethered to the technology hubs in East Asia and North America. Nokia's slide since 2008 highlights the pitfalls for a company specializing in a narrow product range and the risks for a country that relies heavily on a single firm—or a few firms[11]—that has weak input-output (I-O) links with the rest of the economy for production, exports, and innovation.[12]

MNCs largely account for Ireland's recent industrialization and for Singapore's as well, but to attract the MNCs, both countries have had to offer a generous package of tax and other incentives.[13] Ireland's efforts to repair its finances following the global crisis of 2008 to 2009 are affected by the low 12.5 percent corporate income tax rate, which MNCs view as indispensable to the viability of their

---

[11]The Republic of Korea's fortunes are tied to a handful of large conglomerates that dominate the export and technology sectors and exercise enormous political leverage.

[12]Daveri and Silva (2004, 148) observe that "Nokia is relatively unconnected in the I-O sense with the rest of the economy. Finland's greater reliance on the slower-growing EU and Russian markets might also be affecting its performance since 2008." Similar worries regarding reliance on the technological prowess of one or a few firms have also surfaced in Korea in connection with the innovativeness of the smart phones produced by Samsung (Ihlwan 2010).

[13]Honohan and Walsh (2002) stress Ireland's low corporate income tax rates, grant assistance to MNCs, and freedom to repatriate profits, all of which have brought FDI into mature capital-intensive industries producing enormously profitable patented products (especially pharmaceuticals, microprocessors, software, and food products).

operations. FDI transfers technology, with vertical transfers being more common than horizontal diffusion. This situation is a plus, but MNCs have contributed little to the creation and growth of indigenous firms in either Ireland or Singapore, and the banyan tree effect has been viewed by policy makers in these countries as a disadvantage.[14]

In fact, the Sifire countries lack a sufficiently dynamic small and medium-size enterprise (SME) sector, which can provide a seedbed for larger world-class firms and churn the business sector to continuously refresh the top tier of national firms (see Haltiwanger 2008). Other countries also lack dynamic SME sectors, including Malaysia and South Africa, both of which host numerous MNCs. Thus, the message on this score is equivocal: with the exception of the Republic of Korea; Taiwan, China; and possibly Finland, all the other late-blooming small economies have ridden the coattails of MNCs.

For several countries, this route has been advantageous, but MNCs are unreliable growth engines over the long term. They are continually scanning the horizon for less costly production platforms to enhance their returns. They are likely to absorb the cream of the local technical and managerial talent and often funnel out the best to their international operations. They are less likely to engage in fundamental research, preferring to limit themselves to adaptation of products for local markets and some applied research and testing. MNCs prefer to rely on technology transfers from their core research centers and on the trusted suppliers with a global reach. They do not actively assist the country in building indigenous entrepreneurship or augment the flora of local firms.

The problem for many late-starting countries is that in a world straddled by buyer- or supplier-controlled value chains (Gereffi 1996, 2001), countries need large MNCs, whether home grown or foreign, to link with these chains and establish a foothold in the global market. But MNCs can be unreliable partners over the long haul, especially for countries with small domestic markets.[15] Large economies such as China and India are the ones most attractive to MNCs, even in relation to the advanced Western ones, because their size and growth prospects hold the most promise. Moreover, these countries are creating their own MNCs and building up research capabilities that rival those of the advanced economies, with the benefit of wages of technical workers that are a fraction of those in Sifire or, for that matter, in the United States.

---

[14]The *banyan tree effect* occurs when MNCs favor their own traditional suppliers, tend to absorb a lot of the best local talent, and are quick to take over promising local start-ups, with the result that the local SME sector does not become dense. But see footnote 6.

[15]A consolidation of value chains is tightening the links among current participants but threatens to further marginalize potential suppliers on the periphery (Canuto and Salazar 2010).

Under these circumstances, an effective central planning and coordinating body can build a favorable investment climate and orient economic activities to maximize the growth potential deriving from productivity and technological change. Parallel attention to policy implementation capabilities enhances the speed of response. Sifire's recovery from crises in the 1980s and performance through the 1990s highlight the quality of government. Sifire seized opportunities and grew because the three countries had begun crafting the institutions and networks essential to the conduct of effective policy. By empowering these institutions and using networks, governments were able to pursue objectives with the coordinated support of key stakeholders. Rapid and efficient implementation of policies creates a virtuous spiral. People can see that public agencies are delivering on their promises; they can see positive results. Such a climate legitimizes government, adds to political capital, and energizes as well as expands networks within the country. Public sector efficiency and national economic performance also build an international reputation—they embellish the country's brand—thereby providing an inducement for foreign businesses.

In just a decade, the Sifire countries were being touted as economic icons—small resource-poor countries that had elbowed their way forward by dint of clever policy making and systematic application of human talent. The global crisis of 2008 to 2009 and subsequent decline in economic performance have revealed flaws and gaps in the Sifire model. For example, in Finland, coordination across ministries and the involvement of the Finance Ministry in innovation policy making are deemed inadequate, the procedures for evaluating programs lack sufficient independence and objectivity, and high-tech start-up activity and scaling up of SMEs falls well short of expectations. Such gaps do not diminish the attractiveness of the model; they only show that, as with everything, there is always room for improvement. Crises shine a spotlight on weaknesses and create an opening for reforms.

Almost all late starters have their own planning agencies, but all too frequently these agencies do not muster much political clout, technical expertise, or administrative leverage. In some cases, for legacy reasons, a moribund agency can be difficult to revive and endow with substantial authority and technical capabilities. But given the political will, bringing such agencies to life is by no means impossible. Much depends on who is appointed to head the agency and the connections that person has with other key players in the economic hierarchy and the country's leadership. The success of planning bodies in Taiwan, China, rested on the standing and influence of the people who directed economic management in the 1970s and 1980s. There are risks associated with vesting too much power in a single agency, because it can aggressively pursue misguided objectives and silence criticism. There are plenty of instances from around the world of this problem occurring, including in Indonesia and Korea. However, given the options, which are few, attempting to create a lead agency and building that agency's technical, coordinating, and implementation capabilities are good bets.

Quality of Human Capital

Human capital of high quality emerged as one of the principal drivers in Sifire, but only after the policy-making institutions and networks had begun gaining traction. These policy makers defined the goals for the education system and served to mesh the workings of schools and universities with the rest of the economy. Undoubtedly, the smallness of these three countries and the concentration of most of the training facilities in a few cities magnified the power of networks, thereby making it easier to devise as well as implement policies.

Finland and Singapore have shown that there are different roads to a quality education, but teachers and their incentives are central to both countries, as is the culture of excellence in motivating parents, students, and schools. It is unclear whether a centralized school system, free schooling, school autonomy, time devoted to instruction, and a large volume of homework were important in themselves, though in some combination these conditions may have reinforced the effectiveness of teachers and of the learning systems.[16] Aiming for a high average level of quality for the student body and instilling basic scientific literacy enhanced the productivity of the workforce, as did the successful inducing of a high percentage of students to study science and engineering.

Having put the schooling system on a sound footing, Sifire showed tremendous initiative in expanding tertiary institutions without compromising quality.[17] The big test was to find staff members of sufficient caliber for the newly created universities and polytechnics. Some of the best graduates had to be persuaded to become teachers and researchers, which meant paying high salaries, providing an attractive well-equipped work environment, and according faculty social recognition. This same challenge faces late starters in South Asia and in Sub-Saharan Africa.

Before the 1980s, Sifire had made some progress toward modern learning systems. However, the conditions prevailing in the 1980s—the crises, globalization, technological revolutions, the implosion of the Soviet Union, and so forth—prompted strategic rethinking in Sifire, stoked economic activity, and underscored the imperative of a world-class learning economy.

Looking ahead, one finds that the role of learning and research to drive innovation is undiminished; if anything, future growth is more tightly linked to productivity gains deriving from education. But the Sifire countries will have a hard time

---

[16]See the discussion of decentralized school management and teacher incentives in Bruns, Filmer, and Patrinos (2010).

[17]International experience—mainly U.S.-based—suggests that universities are more productive when they have greater autonomy and are exposed to competition (Aghion and others 2010). See also the survey of findings in Yusuf, Saint, and Nabeshima (2009). Universities in Sifire were exposed to some competition from local and overseas institutions, but probably to a lesser degree than occurred in the United States.

sustaining all but very high-end manufacturing activities in the face of competition from Asian countries. Tradable services are becoming exposed to equally intense pressure from overseas suppliers. In response, Singapore is actively diversifying its productive base, attempting to hold on to as many manufacturing industries as it can while promoting other activities—mainly high-value services and tourism.[18] Finland and Ireland need to follow suit. To successfully diversify into other high-value adding activities, Sifire countries will need to reshape their learning systems to sustain math and science skills while helping students improve their noncognitive skills and become more creative. The advent of the Internet and social networking has created an immensity of electronic noise and innumerable diversions that are dividing the attention of students and eroding disciplined study habits and interest in sustained reading. This electronic noise also makes it difficult to deepen writing skills. Teachers have to strive harder to convey the "process of science"; the "deep connections between the core disciplines of physics, chemistry, and biology"; and the "excitement and beauty of the scientific view of how the world works" (Lederman 2008, 399). The Internet, video games, and television are helping to develop the visual intelligence of young people, but at the cost of other cognitive skills. The "cost seems to be deep processing: mindful knowledge acquisition, inductive analysis, critical thinking, imagination, and reflection"—attributes that society needs more than ever (Greenfield 2009, 71).

To accommodate the shifting demands of employers, training institutions are having to use greater foresight to ascertain the future composition of desired skills and adjust their course offerings accordingly to minimize skill mismatches. The significance of feedback from employers and of networking is becoming greater than ever, although the willingness of footloose MNCs to invest in local human capital and innovation systems is questionable.

With accumulating knowledge, the STEM disciplines are steadily becoming more demanding in terms of the quantum of knowledge that must be assimilated and the analytical skill required to solve complex problems. Consequently, fewer tertiary-level students are willing to invest the time and effort. The percentage of students majoring in science and engineering is declining in Sifire countries as it is almost worldwide. This trend risks weakening hard-won technological and innovation capabilities. To reverse the trend, government and businesses will have to redouble their joint efforts to shore up incentives (including incentives to finance training) and to provide rewarding career prospects to people who graduate with science and engineering degrees.

The steady buildup of knowledge in every disciplinary field and the interdisciplinary content of many products and services mean that all but the very largest

---

[18]The Marina Bay Sands Casino, which was built at a cost of US$5.5 billion (the second most costly complex of its type in the world), represents Singapore's efforts to diversify. Built by Las Vegas Sands Corp., the complex reaffirms the role of FDI in the services industry.

countries must necessarily specialize. Firms and researchers need to network and collaborate with their counterparts in other countries, thus exploiting the open global innovation system. Ireland's attempt to reignite the growth of Silicon Dock in Dublin, Finland's struggle to remain a world-class supplier of telecommunication equipment, and Singapore's ongoing efforts to become a biotech hotspot[19] highlight the challenge for small countries far removed from the established centers of excellence to carve out a place for themselves. At the same time, Singapore has demonstrated its ability to attract world-class researchers[20] to its recently established biotech research center and enlarge its tertiary education system in partnership with leading European and U.S. universities. This example shows how late starters can tap the pool of international knowledge workers to augment and groom local talent.[21] Late-starting countries confront even sterner challenges, which could be compounded by a weakening of globalization or if globalization takes a different turn in a multipolar world. Stevens, Miller, and Michalski (2000, 16) caution that globalization could widen social differences:

> Globalisation's dependence on and reinforcement of differences is at the origin of much concern about its social consequences.... First,... the world has no mechanisms that enable those who win because of change to compensate those who lose. Secondly, and this difficulty is related to the first, without the infrastructure needed to overcome exclusion there is a great risk that globalisation's social heterogeneity will turn into destabilisingly high levels of fragmentation and polarization.[22]

Implications for African Countries

Small, resource-poor economies may need to try harder, but firmly adhering to a high-growth strategy and creating the governance institutions, human

---

[19]See Normile (2002) for a listing of the measures Singapore had taken to create an infrastructure of institutes supporting training and hospital facilities and to attract foreign researchers and companies.

[20]Most of the principal researchers at the Institute of Molecular and Cell Biology, created in 1987, were recruited from overseas.

[21]Singapore began building Biopolis—a bioscience city—and the Tuas Biomedical Park in 2003. Although several MNCs have set research facilities in the space provided, there is as yet little evidence that Singapore is on the way to creating a cluster rivaling Medicon Valley in Denmark, much less the clusters in Boston and San Diego. See Normile (2002) and Yusuf and Nabeshima (2006). However, Singapore has aggressively pursued the development of additional science parks with the building of Fusionopolis to spur multimedia-related businesses. The latest initiative is One North, a 200-hectare park for biomed, IT, and multimedia companies that is visualized as the axis of Singapore's science hub (Engardio 2009).

[22]Kemeny (2011) notes that the technology gap between the most and the least developed economies grew between 1972 and 2001. The most sophisticated economies may continue to pull further away from the least, thereby setting the stage for greater polarization along several axes.

capital, and urban-industrial-research networking such a strategy entails is a proven way forward. The scope for technological catch-up offers the opportunity, and an efficiently governed learning economy provides a means of closing the gap. The Sifire countries provide a model of compressed development. Proven alternatives are difficult to identify from cross-country experience spanning the past half-century. However, as with any strategy, the Sifire model will need to be adapted by late starters to account for changed global conditions and unique country circumstances. African and other low-income economies in search of ways to accelerate growth must, at the minimum, factor in the following:

- Sifire transitioned toward the phase of rapid industrialization and growth from a more advanced level of development than many of the current low-income countries. The Sifire group's industrial capabilities in the 1980s were of a higher order, as was the group's human capital. The Sifire countries were better prepared to absorb technology and to exploit advances in scientific knowledge. And they already had a stratum of well-educated people from which to recruit the teachers needed to nurture technical skills.

- Globalization, the electronics and the information technology (IT) revolution, and the offshoring of industry from the United States and other advanced countries favored all three countries to varying degrees. Now entry barriers to the electronics and IT sectors are higher for newcomers. Late-starting countries need to quickly muster substantial manufacturing and technological capabilities if they are to compete on the basis of price and quality with seasoned suppliers who already enjoy cost and learning advantages.[23] These advantages accrue from links with established value chains. The speed at which products are imitated and rents competed away is also a handicap for newcomers hoping to carve out profitable niches. For a wide range of manufactured products, the barriers to entry for existing producers are now quite low, and this ease of diversification raises the odds against newcomers.

- The Sifire countries did not confront the challenges posed by competition from China and, to a lesser extent, India through much of the 1990s. They faced competition from other countries, but it was nowhere near as fierce as the threat Chinese manufacturers and Indian IT service providers now present. Some research suggests that the development of skills in African countries may be inhibited by the import of skill-intensive products, which slow the indigenous upgrading of production and maintain, if not widen, the income divergence between Sub-Saharan Africa and the rest of the world (Auer 2010).

---

[23]For a number of industries, wage costs are dwarfed by other costs eroding the advantages bestowed by low-wage labor.

- Energy and resource scarcities[24] and environmental concerns were not as pressing or inhibiting to growth.
- Global growth prospects were robust even though the economic performance of Sub-Saharan Africa and Latin America was lagging. Demand from the advanced countries was strong and became stronger in the 1990s.[25] Following the global crisis of 2008 to 2009 and the longer-term adjustment imperatives of major economies in the Organisation for Economic Co-operation and Development, global demand for the exports of industrializing countries could be significantly weaker.[26] At the same time, the performance of Sub-Saharan Africa is much superior to what it was in the 1990s. GDP rose by an average of 4.9 percent a year between 2000 and 2009, the future prognosis is more positive than in the 1990s, and portfolio and FDI are flowing to the continent (see McKinsey Global Institute 2010). But the performance remains a function of strong and rising prices of raw materials and investment in infrastructure to develop these resources. The domestic beneficiation of mineral resources remains low even in relatively industrial nations such as South Africa. Although South-South trade is picking up, with Sub-Saharan Africa exporting more to China, the technology level of these exports is lower than that of the exports by African countries to the West.

These changed circumstances, if anything, enhance the attractiveness of the Sifire model for late starters and middle-income countries: the importance of technology as a driver of growth has risen, and so also has the skill intensity of technologies. Absorbing and fully harnessing technologies makes it essential to aim high in building a learning economy. Late starters can also usefully reconsider the approach to innovation by focusing on cost innovation and aiming for lower-income buyers closer to the bottom of the pyramid. With the

---

[24]Opinions vary on this issue, with one side pointing to the disparities between the growth trend in the supplies of fuels (and net exports of oil and condensates) and other minerals and the growth in demand, especially from industrializing Asian countries. The other side points to long-term stable or declining price trends and technological advances that contribute to the elasticity of supply and provide substitutes for resources as they grow scarce.

[25]The East Asian crisis of 1997 to 1998 and the deflating of the dot-com bubble slowed, but did not derail the growth of the three economies.

[26]The overhang of fiscal and trade imbalances bedeviling several of the major economies threatens a slowing or partial reversal of globalization (Oxford Analytica 2010b). As long as essentially short-term political calculations prevent governments from taking ultimately unavoidable action, the future of globalization will remain clouded. Hufbauer and Suominen (2010) point out that climate change and national security are compounding the threat.

fastest-growing markets now located in industrializing countries such as China and India and in regions such as Southeast Asia and Sub-Saharan Africa, low-tech innovation[27] could offer better market prospects in an era of increasing South-South trade and be more attuned to the capabilities of late starters.[28] Thus a more creative approach to innovation is called for—not necessarily the one adopted by Sifire. Also, unlike Sifire countries, which invested very little in research and development (R&D) during the 1960s and 1970s, the late starters may need to complement investment in tertiary education with incentives for R&D to improve the quality of higher-level skills, speed up the assimilation of technology, and lay the groundwork for indigenous innovation. Ireland, which has devoted far fewer resources to R&D than have Finland and Singapore, is now paying the price for neglect.[29] By absorbing technologies faster and building capacity for innovation, late starters can begin to broaden their capabilities. These capabilities will be vital for diversifying their economies and climbing out of low-level industrial and primary production traps (Hausmann and Hidalgo 2010). Countries in Sub-Saharan Africa may need to explore the scope for innovating in services, where the opportunities might be richer, easier, and cheaper to commercialize and also easier to scale up.[30] The smallness of these countries will necessarily will mean that they must start by combining teaching and research and by focusing resources and talent on a few promising areas until more trained personnel are available. International institutions and major foreign universities might provide some support, but experience suggests that this assistance will be minimal. Countries will have to be more self-reliant.

A big change from the 1990s may be that South-South trade, capital, and technology flows become far more important and faster growing, with countries such as China emerging as major importers and suppliers of capital and technology.[31]

---

[27]Such innovation is off to a slow start in Africa. In the area of health, for example, identifying new drugs, medical devices, and equipment is proceeding slowly with little commercialization, partly because of the shortage of venture finance (Simiyu, Daar, and Singer 2010).

[28]Although frequently touted, the so-called inclusive low-tech innovations targeting the poor are few in number and are insufficiently scalable. Moreover, these innovations have attracted little venture financing and have yet to demonstrate their macroeconomic potential. See Oxford Analytica (2010c).

[29]Ireland is seeking to protect its research budget from the draconian cuts of expenditures forced by the financial crisis (Gilbert 2010).

[30]Innovation in services might benefit from the "open" approach proposed by Henry Chesbrough. See Chesbrough (2011) for many illuminating examples of pathways to innovation in services.

[31]As discussed previously, Sub-Saharan Africa's exports to China consist of commodities and semiprocessed products, and imports of low-cost Chinese manufactures confront local producers with severe challenges.

This factor will undoubtedly affect development strategy,[32] industrialization, the export mix, and technological development. Only time will tell whether, on balance, this shift in the global economic center of gravity will be good for late starters.

Despite how globalization evolves, small economies in Sub-Saharan Africa, would benefit from access to a Pan-African market with few barriers. Finland and Ireland gained from the formation of a common market. The gains to all members of the EU would be even greater today if the plethora of laws, standards, tax codes, and intellectual property rules were replaced by uniform institutions.[33] For Africa, market integration is a long-running project, but it is a project that is taking on more urgency as the world economy steers into uncharted waters. As Michael Porter (1998) noted in *The Competitive Advantage of Nations*, the size and sophistication of markets profoundly stimulate both competitiveness and innovation, thereby forcing firms to upgrade and offer new and higher-quality products. The greater the willingness of consumers to demand and to use new products is, the greater the incentives for firms to satisfy these demands will be.[34]

Whether countries hew to a Sifire-type strategy or choose a different approach, the outcome will be crucially linked to design, planning, institutional architecture, and implementation. The efficacy of these elements will be affected by governance mechanisms.[35] In part, such mechanisms are a function of domestic politics, about which this book says little. But the Sifire countries have much to teach developing countries about how to enhance the efficiency of governance institutions, how to contribute to productivity and innovation by harnessing IT, and how to avoid some of the pitfalls. A small example must suffice: Finland has taken the lead in introducing electronic invoicing to eliminate a vast number of costly

---

[32]References to the still-nebulous Beijing Consensus and the revival of interest in industrial strategy suggest that the developmental state might be back in favor, although it could be a softer and more flexible state than the rigid type that is so much a part of East Asian legend. If so, the Sifire experience could provide useful pointers.

[33]This situation is spelled out in the call for a single market contained in a report prepared for the European Commission by Mario Monti (2010). The prospect seems even more distant in 2012.

[34]Bhidé (2006) ascribes the innovativeness of U.S. firms to the venturesome behavior of consumers and the vast U.S. domestic market.

[35]One indicator of governance that emerges from the World Bank's Doing Business survey is not encouraging. The latest report (2011), which is available at http://www .doingbusiness.org, shows that of the 50 lowest-ranked countries, 32 were from Sub-Saharan Africa. Of these 32, 15 had experienced a decline in their ranking over the preceding year. According to a second indicator, the Afrobarometer, which is available at http://www.afrobarometer.org, satisfaction with democratic performance diminished in the 11 countries tracked by the surveys from 1999 through 2008. See Gilley (2010).

paper transactions and to facilitate a variety of transactions, from shopping to the payment of pensions. Finnish mobile phone operators are issuing individuals with electronic IDs that can be used for a wide range of purposes. These innovations will feed into Finland's bottom line through productivity, and they will do so more speedily if the population is better educated.

References

Aghion, Philippe, Mathias Dewatripont, Caroline M. Hoxby, Andreu Mas-Collel, and André Sapir. 2010. "The Governance and Performance of Universities: Evidence from Europe and the U.S." *Economic Policy* 25 (61) 7–59.

Auer, Raphael. 2010. "Are Imports from Rich Nations Deskilling Emerging Economies? Human Capital and the Dynamic Effects of Trade." Working Paper 2010-18, Swiss National Bank, Zurich.

Bhidé, Amar. 2006. "Venturesome Consumption, Innovation, and Globalization." Paper for the Joint Conference of CESifo and the Center on Capitalism and Society on Perspectives on the Performance of the Continent's Economies, Venice, Italy, July 21–22.

Breznitz, Shiri M., and Antti-Jussi Tahvanainen. 2010. "Cluster Sustainability in Peripheral Regions: A Case Study on Israel's and Finland's Biotechnology Industries." Discussion Paper 1212, Research Institute of the Finnish Economy, Helsinki.

Bruns, Barbara, Deon Filmer, and Harry Anthony Patrinos. 2010. "Making Schools Work: New Evidence on Accountability Reforms." Mimeo. World Bank, Washington, DC.

Brynjolfsson, Erik, and Andrew McAfee. 2011. *Race against the Machine: How the Digital Revolution Is Accelerating Innovation, Driving Productivity, and Irreversibly Transforming Employment and the Economy.* Lexington, MA: Digital Frontier Press.

Canuto, Otaviano, and José Manuel Salazar. 2010. "Challenges in the Coming Phase of Globalisation: A Sense of Déjà Vu." VoxEU.org, June 28.

Chesbrough, Henry. 2011. *Open Services Innovation: Rethinking Your Business to Grow and Compete in a New Era.* San Francisco, CA: Jossey-Bass.

Daveri, Francesco, and Olmo Silva. 2004. "Not Only Nokia: What Finland Tells Us about New Economy Growth." *Economic Policy* 19 (38): 117–63.

Engardio, Pete. 2009. "Singapore's One North." *Bloomberg Businessweek*, June 1. http://www.businessweek.com/innovate/content/jun2009/id2009061_019963.htm.

Ford, Martin. 2009. *The Lights in the Tunnel: Automation, Accelerating Technology, and the Economy of the Future.* Acculant Publishing.

Foster, Robert Fitzroy. 2008. *Luck and the Irish: A Brief History of Change from 1970.* Oxford, U.K.: Oxford University Press.

Gereffi, Gary. 1996. "Global Commodity Chains: New Forms of Coordination and Control among Nations and Firms in International Industries." *Competition and Change* 1 (4): 427–39.

———. 2001. "Beyond the Producer-Driven/Buyer-Driven Dichotomy: The Evolution of Global Value Chains in the Internet Era. *IDS Bulletin.* 32 (3): 30–40.

Gilbert, Natasha. 2010. "Ireland Defends Research from Cuts." *Nature* 467: 895. http://www.nature.com/news/2010/101019/full/467895a.html.

Gilley, Bruce. 2010. "The End of the African Renaissance." *Washington Quarterly* 33 (4): 87–101.

Görg, Holger, Aoife Hanley, and Eric Strobl. 2010. "FDI in Ireland: New Findings for Grants and Local Partnerships." VoxEU.org, October 5. http://www.voxeu.org/index.php?q=node/5619.

Greenfield, Patricia. 2009. "Technology and Informal Education: What Is Taught, What Is Learned." *Science* 323 (3): 69–71.

Haltiwanger, John. 2008. "The Dynamics of Young Businesses: Importance for Growth and Measurement Challenges." Keynote address at the Kauffman Foundation Conference on Entrepreneurship and Innovation Data, Copenhagen, May 28–29. http://www.oecd.org/dataoecd/34/48/40808184.pdf.

Hausmann, Ricardo, and César A. Hidalgo. 2010. "Country Diversification, Product Ubiquity, and Economic Divergence." Working Paper Series 10-045, John F. Kennedy School of Government, Harvard University, Cambridge, MA.

HelsinginSanomat. 2004. "ETLA Sees No Sign of Investment-Driven Growth." *Helsingin-Sanomat*, June 4.

Hirschman, Albert O. 1970. *Exit, Voice, and Loyalty: Responses to Decline in Firms, Organizations, and States*. Cambridge, MA: Harvard University Press.

Honohan, Patrick, and Brendan Walsh. 2002. "Catching Up with the Leaders: The Irish Hare." *Brookings Papers on Economic Activity* 33 (1): 1–78.

Hufbauer, Gary, and Kati Suominen. 2010. *Globalization at Risk: Challenges to Finance and Trade*. New Haven, CT: Yale University Press.

Ihlwan, Moon. 2010. "Korean Tech Is Losing Its Cool: How Korea, a Onetime Digital Trendsetter, Became a Laggard in an Era of Smartphones—and Amazing Apps." 2010. *Bloomberg Businessweek*, February 17. http://www.businessweek.com/magazine/content/10_09/b4168024781121.htm.

Kemeny, Thomas. 2011. "Are International Technology Gaps Growing or Shrinking in the Age of Globalization?" *Journal of Economic Geography* 11 (1): 1–35.

Lederman, Leon M. 2008. "Scientists and 21st Century Science Education." *Technology in Society* 30 (3–4): 397–400.

Lewis, Michael. 2011. "When Irish Eyes Are Crying." *Vanity Fair*, March. http://www.vanityfair.com/business/features/2011/03/michael-lewis-ireland-201103.

Lynn, Matthew. 2010. "The Fallen King of Finland." *Bloomberg Businessweek*, September 20.

McKinsey Global Institute. 2010. "Lions on the Move: The Progress and Potential of African Economies." McKinsey & Company, Washington, DC.

Monti, Mario. 2010. *A New Strategy for the Single Market: At the Service of Europe's Economy and Society*. Brussels: European Commission. http://ec.europa.eu/bepa/pdf/monti_report_final_10_05_2010_en.pdf.

Mutalib, Hussin. 2000. "Constitutional-Electoral Reforms and Politics in Singapore." *Legislative Studies Quarterly* 27 (4): 659–72

———. 2003. *Parties and Politics: A Study of Opposition Parties and the PAP in Singapore*. Singapore: Eastern Universities Press.

Normile, Dennis. 2002. "Can Money Turn Singapore into a Biotech Juggernaut." *Science* 297 (5586): 1470–73.

Oxford Analytica. 2008. "Singapore: Export Slump Hits Growth." Oxford Analytica, October 8.

———. 2010a. "Finland: Growth Depends on Competitiveness and Exports." Oxford Analytica, March 30.

———. 2010b. "International: Globalisation Could Be Reversed." Oxford Analytica, December 21.

———. 2010c. "International: Impact Investment Grows, Faces Hurdles." Oxford Analytica, August 16.

———. 2010d. "Singapore: Global Economic Volatility Weighs on Growth." Oxford Analytica, November 16.

Parker, Andrew, and Andrew Ward. 2011. "Downwardly Mobile." *Financial Times*, February 25.

Porter, Michael E. 1998. *The Competitive Advantage of Nations*. New York: Free Press.

Portes, Richard. 2011. "Restructure Ireland's Debt." VoxEU.org, April 26. http://www.voxeu.org/index.php?q=node/6380.

Rodan, Garry. 2006. "Singapore 'Exceptionalism'? Authoritarian Rule and State Transformation." In *Political Transitions in Dominant Party Systems: Learning to Lose*, ed. Edward Friedman and Joseph Wong, 231–51. Abingdon, U.K.: Routledge.

Simiyu, Ken, Abdallah S. Daar, and Peter A. Singer. 2010. "Stagnant Health Technologies in Africa." *Science* 330 (6010): 1483–84.

Stevens, Barrie, Riel Miller, and Wolfgang Michalski. 2000. "Social Diversity and the Creative Society of the 21st Century." In *The Creative Society of the 21st Century*, 7–24. Paris: Organisation for Economic Co-operation and Development.

Toner, Phillip. 2011. "Workforce Skills and Innovation: An Overview of Major Themes in the Literature." Organisation for Economic Co-operation and Development, Paris.

Uzzi, Brian, and Jarrett Spiro. 2005. "Collaboration and Creativity: The Small World Problem." *American Journal of Sociology* 111 (2): 447–504.

Yusuf, Shahid, and Kaoru Nabeshima. 2006. *Post-industrial East Asian Cities*. Palo Alto, CA: Stanford University Press.

Yusuf, Shahid, William Saint, and Kaoru Nabeshima. 2009. *Accelerating Catch-up: Tertiary Education for Growth in Sub-Saharan Africa*. Washington, DC: World Bank.

Zakaria, Fareed. 1997. "The Rise of Illiberal Democracy." *Foreign Affairs*, November–December.

Appendix A

Table A.1 Ghana's Top Five Exports

	1996			2007	
Product name	**Trade value (US$ million)**	**Technology class**	**Product name**	**Trade value (US$ million)**	**Technology class**
Beans, whole or broken, raw	748	PP	Gold, nonmonetary	1,459	LT2
Gold, nonmonetary	740	LT2	Beans, whole or broken, raw	896	PP
Wood of nonconiferous species, sawn	212	RB1	Wood of nonconiferous species, sawn	154	RB1
Wood, sawn lengthwise, sliced or peeled	169	RB1	Cocoa butter and cocoa paste	148	PP
Cocoa butter and cocoa paste	115	PP	Wood, sawn lengthwise, sliced or peeled	73	RB1

Source: United Nations Commodity Trade Statistics Database.
Note: LT2 = other low-technology products; PP = primary products; RB1 = agriculture-based products.

Table A.2 Kenya's Top Five Exports

	1995			2007	
Product name	**Trade value (US$ million)**	**Technology class**	**Product name**	**Trade value (US$ million)**	**Technology class**
Tea	362	PP	Tea	698	PP
Coffee, whether or not roasted	292	PP	Cut flowers and foliage	390	PP
Cut flowers and foliage	68	PP	Other fresh or chilled vegetables	232	PP

(continued on next page)

Table A.2 *(continued)*

1995			2007		
Product name	Trade value (US$ million)	Technology class	Product name	Trade value (US$ million)	Technology class
Other sheets and plates of iron	66	LT2	Coffee, whether or not roasted	165	PP
Fruit, otherwise prepared or preserved	54	RB1	Cigarettes	94	RB1

Source: United Nations Commodity Trade Statistics Database.
Note: LT2 = other low-technology products; PP = primary products; RB1 = agriculture-based products.

Table A.3   South Africa's Top Five Exports

1996			2007		
Product name	Trade value (US$ million)	Technology class	Product name	Trade value (US$ million)	Technology class
Beans, whole or broken, raw	748	PP	Gold, nonmonetary	1,459	LT2
Gold, nonmonetary	740	LT2	Beans, whole or broken, raw	896	PP
Wood of nonconiferous species, sawn	212	RB1	Wood of nonconiferous species, sawn	154	RB1
Wood, sawn lengthwise, sliced or peeled	169	RB1	Cocoa butter and cocoa paste	148	PP
Cocoa butter and cocoa paste	115	PP	Wood, sawn lengthwise, sliced or peeled	73	RB1

Source: United Nations Commodity Trade Statistics Database.
Note: LT2 = other low-technology products; PP = primary products; RB1 = agriculture-based products.

Table A.4   Rwanda's Top Five Exports

1996			2007		
Product name	Trade value (US$ million)	Technology class	Product name	Trade value (US$ million)	Technology class
Coffee, whether or not roasted	4	PP	Ores and concentrates of other nonferrous base metals	43	RB2
Tea	1	PP	Tin ores and concentrates	39	RB2
Motor vehicles for transport of goods	1	MT1	Coffee, whether or not roasted	32	PP
Tin ores and concentrates	1	RB2	Tea	30	PP
Calfskins, raw (fresh, salted, dried)	1	PP	Passenger motorcars, for transport	4	MT1

Source: United Nations Commodity Trade Statistics Database.
Note: MT1 = automotive products; PP = primary products; RB2 = resource-based products.

Table A.5   Zambia's Top Five Exports

	1995			2007	
Product name	Trade value (US$ million)	Technology class	Product name	Trade value (US$ million)	Technology class
Copper and copper alloys, refined or not	856	PP	Copper and copper alloys, refined or not	2,257	PP
Cotton yarn	30	LT1	Copper and copper alloys, worked	1,023	PP
Copper and copper alloys, worked	28	PP	Copper ores and concentrates; copper matte	256	RB2
Electric current	26	RB2	Semimanufactures of tungsten, molybdenum	249	LT2
Sugars, beet and cane, raw, solid	17	RB1	Sugars, beet and cane, raw, solid	82	RB1

Source: United Nations Commodity Trade Statistics Database.
Note: LT1 = textiles and fashion products; LT2 = other low-technology products; PP = primary products; RB1 = agriculture-based products; RB2 = resource-based products.

Table A.6   Costa Rica's Top Five Exports

	1996			2009	
Product name	Trade value (US$ million)	Technology class	Product name	Trade value (US$ million)	Technology class
Bananas, including plantains, fresh	687	PP	Parts and accessories of data-processing equipment not elsewhere specified	857	HT1
Coffee, not roasted or decaffeinated	417	PP	Monolithic integrated circuits, digital	663	HT1
Pineapples, fresh or dried	59	PP	Bananas, including plantains, fresh	448	PP
Raw cane sugar, in solid form	46	RB1	Pineapples, fresh or dried	445	PP
Melons and watermelons, fresh	46	PP	Needles, catheters, cannulae, and so forth (medical)	378	MT3

Source: United Nations Commodity Trade Statistics Database.
Note: HT1 = electronics and electrical products; MT3 = engineering products; PP = primary products; RB1 = agriculture-based products.

Table A.7   Jordan's Top Five Exports

	1995			2009	
Product name	Trade value (US$ million)	Technology class	Product name	Trade value (US$ million)	Technology class
Vegetable fats, oils, or fractions hydrogenated, esterified	200	RB1	Potassic fertilizers, mixes, not elsewhere specified (pack > 10 kilograms)	447	MT2
Carnallite, sylvite, and other crude natural potassium salts	173	PP	Unground natural calcium phosphates	372	PP
Nitrogenous fertilizers, mixes, not elsewhere specified (pack > 10 kilograms)	157	MT2	Medicaments not elsewhere specified, in dosage	352	HT2
Unground natural calcium phosphates	150	PP	Garments not elsewhere specified, of cotton, knit	323	LT1
Medicaments not elsewhere specified, in dosage	113	HT2	Nitrogenous fertilizers, mixes, not elsewhere specified (pack > 10 kilograms)	206	MT2

Source: United Nations Commodity Trade Statistics Database.
Note: HT2 = other high-technology products; LT1 = textiles and fashion products; MT2 = process industries (chemicals and basic metals); PP = primary products; RB1 = agriculture-based products.

Table A.8   Mauritius's Top Five Exports

	1995			2009	
Product name	Trade value (US$ million)	Technology class	Product name	Trade value (US$ million)	Technology class
Raw cane sugar, in solid form	364	RB1	T-shirts, singlets, and other vests	252	LT1
T-shirts, singlets, and other vests	202	LT1	Raw cane sugar, in solid form	215	RB1
Men's or boys' shirts of cotton	123	LT1	Tuna, skipjack, and bonito, prepared or preserved, not minced	211	RB1
Men's or boys' trousers, breeches	78	LT1	Men's or boys' shirts of cotton	106	LT1
Jerseys, pullovers, and so forth, of wool	73	LT1	Men's or boys' trousers, breeches	78	LT1

Source: United Nations Commodity Trade Statistics Database.
Note: LT1 = textiles and fashion products; RB1 = agriculture-based products.

Table A.9   Morocco's Top Five Exports

	1995			2009	
Product name	Trade value (US$ million)	Technology class	Product name	Trade value (US$ million)	Technology class
Phosphoric and polyphosphoric acids	551	RB2	Phosphoric and polyphosphoric acids	1,000	RB2
Octopus, frozen, dried, salted, or in brine	297	PP	Unground natural calcium phosphates	643	PP
Unground natural calcium phosphates	285	PP	Ignition wiring sets and other wiring sets	554	MT3
Phosphatic fertilizers, mixes, not elsewhere specified (pack > 10 kilograms)	279	MT2	Transistors, except photosensitive (> 1 watt)	482	HT1
Men's or boys' trousers, breeches	193	LT1	Diammonium phosphate (pack > 10 kilograms)	429	MT2

Source: United Nations Commodity Trade Statistics Database.
Note: HT1 = electronics and electrical products; LT1 = textiles and fashion products; MT2 = process industries (chemicals and basic metals); MT3 = engineering products; PP = primary products; RB2 = resource-based products.

Table A.10   Tunisia's Top Five Exports

	1995			2009	
Product name	Trade value (US$ million)	Technology class	Product name	Trade value (US$ million)	Technology class
Men's or boys' trousers, breeches	582	LT1	Petroleum oils, oils from bituminous minerals, crude	1,550	PP
Petroleum oils, oils from bituminous minerals, crude	378	PP	Electric conductors, not elsewere specified (< 80 volts, with connectors)	555	MT3
Virgin olive oil and fractions	228	RB1	Men's or boys' trousers, breeches	504	LT1
Phosphoric and polyphosphoric acids	202	RB2	Electrical switches, protectors, connecters for < 1 kilovolt, not elsewhere specified	486	MT3
Diammonium phosphate (pack > 10 kilograms)	164	MT2	Petroleum oils and so forth, excluding crude	412	RB2

Source: United Nations Commodity Trade Statistics Database.
Note: LT1 = textiles and fashion products; MT2 = process industries (chemicals and basic metals); MT3 = engineering products; PP = primary products; RB1 = agriculture-based products; RB2 = resource-based products.

Table A.11 Sri Lanka's Top Five Exports

	1994			2009		
Product name	**Trade value (US$ million)**	**Technology class**	**Product name**	**Trade value (US$ million)**	**Technology class**
Tea, black, fermented or partly (pack > 3 kilograms)	256	PP	Tea, black, fermented or partly (pack > 3 kilograms)	662	PP
Tea, black, fermented or partly (pack < 3 kilograms)	159	PP	Tea, black, fermented or partly (pack < 3 kilograms)	485	PP
Diamonds (jewelry), worked but not mounted or set	105	RB2	Brassieres	307	LT1
Precious and semiprecious stones not elsewhere specified, worked, not set	76	RB2	T-shirts, singlets, and other vests	225	LT1
Women's or girls' blouses, shirts	73	LT1	Men's or boys' trousers, breeches	246	LT1

Source: United Nations Commodity Trade Statistics Database.
Note: LT1 = textiles and fashion products; PP = primary products; RB2 = resource-based products.

Appendix B

Table B.1 Finland's Top 10 Exports in 1980, by Value

Rank	Description	Value (US$ million)	Technology class
1	Lumber, sawn, planed, and so forth: conifer	1,321.3	RB1
2	Other printing and writing paper, machine made	1,036.7	RB1
3	Sulfate wood pulp	665.6	RB1
4	Newsprint paper	648.6	RB1
5	Paper and paperboard in rolls or sheets not elsewhere specified	518.9	RB1
6	Ships and boats, other than warships	485.5	MT3
7	Clothing of textile fabric, not knitted or crocheted	452.6	LT1
8	Kraft paper and kraft paperboard	337.1	RB1
9	Plywood, including veneered panels	332.1	RB1
10	Motor spirits, gasoline, and other light oils	300.0	RB2

Source: United Nations Commodity Trade Statistics Database.
Note: LT1 = textiles and fashion products; MT3 = engineering products; RB1 = agriculture-based products; RB2 = resource-based products.

Table B.2 Finland's Top 10 Exports in 1990, by Value

Rank	Description	Value (US$ million)	Technology class
1	Machine made paper and paperboard, simply finished	2,214.6	RB1
2	Other printing and writing paper, machine made	1,592.6	RB1
3	Paper and paperboard in rolls or sheets not elsewhere specified	1,386.3	RB1
4	Lumber, sawn, planed, and so forth: conifer	1,164.1	RB1
5	Telecommunication equipment not elsewhere specified	865.2	HT1
6	Sulfate wood pulp	831.2	RB1
7	Paper mill and pulp mill machinery and so forth	831.1	MT3
8	Newsprint paper	767.2	RB1
9	Kraft paper and kraft paperboard	630.7	RB1
10	Mechanical handling equipment	575.8	MT3

Source: United Nations Commodity Trade Statistics Database.
Note: HT1 = electronics and electrical products; MT3 = engineering products; RB1 = agriculture-based products.

Table B.3 Ireland's Top 10 Exports in 1980, by Value

Rank	Description	Value (US$ million)	Technology class
1	Meat of bovine animals, fresh, chilled, or frozen	957.7	PP
2	Organo-inorganic and heterocyclic compounds	405.8	RB2
3	Statistical machine cards or tapes	350.1	HT1
4	Bovine cattle including buffalo	340.1	PP
5	Butter	259.5	RB1
6	Food preparations not elsewhere specified	253.6	RB1
7	Milk and cream in solid form, blocks, or powder	199.1	PP
8	Office machines, not elsewhere specified	162.6	HT1
9	Medical instruments, not elsewhere specified	137.0	MT3
10	Passenger motorcars, other than buses	121.6	MT1

Source: United Nations Commodity Trade Statistics Database.
Note: HT1 = electronics and electrical products; MT1 = automotive products; MT3 = engineering products; PP = primary products; RB1 = agriculture-based products; RB2 = resource-based products.

Table B.4   Ireland's Top 10 Exports in 1990, by Value

Rank	Description	Value (US$ million)	Technology class
1	Statistical machine cards or tapes	2,505.8	HT1
2	Office machines not elsewhere specified	2,067.0	HT1
3	Phonograph records, recorded tapes, and other sound recordings	1,115.6	LT2
4	Food preparations not elsewhere specified	938.1	RB1
5	Organo-inorganic and heterocyclic compounds	924.6	RB2
6	Meat of bovine animals, fresh, chilled, or frozen	862.6	PP
7	Medicaments	760.4	HT2
8	Nitrogen function compounds	493.7	RB2
9	Medical instruments not elsewhere specified	407.4	MT3
10	Distilled alcoholic beverages	386.8	RB1

Source: United Nations Commodity Trade Statistics Database.
Note: HT1 = electronics and electrical products; HT2 = other high-technology products; LT2 = other low-technology products; MT3 = engineering products; PP = primary products; RB1 = agriculture-based products; RB2 = resource-based products.

Table B.5   Singapore's Top 10 Exports in 1980, by Value

Rank	Description	Value (US$ million)	Technology class
1	Residual fuel oils	1,643.4	RB2
2	Natural rubber and similar natural gums	1,538.8	PP
3	Distillate fuels	1,246.6	RB2
4	Thermionic valves and tubes, transistors, and so forth	1,186.8	HT1
5	Lamp oil and white spirits	980.0	RB2
6	Oils and other products of the distillation of coal tar	710.7	RB2
7	Radio broadcast receivers	643.6	MT3
8	Motor spirits, gasoline, and other light oils	589.2	RB2
9	Telecommunication equipment not elsewhere specified	350.7	HT1
10	Palm oil	304.2	RB1

Source: United Nations Commodity Trade Statistics Database.
Note: HT1 = electronics and electrical products; MT3 = engineering products; PP = primary products; RB1 = agriculture-based products; RB2 = resource-based products.

Table B.6 Singapore's Top 10 Exports in 1990, by Value

Rank	Description	Value (US$ million)	Technology class
1	Statistical machine cards or tapes	6,828.2	HT1
2	Distillate fuels	3,788.6	RB2
3	Thermionic valves and tubes, transistors, and so forth	3,674.6	HT1
4	Telecommunication equipment not elsewhere specified	2,027.5	HT1
5	Office machines not elsewhere specified	2,024.5	HT1
6	Lamp oil and white spirits	1,907.9	RB2
7	Motor spirits, gasoline, and other light oils	1,854.6	RB2
8	Radio broadcast receivers	1,575.9	MT3
9	Phonographs, tape and other sound recorders, and so forth	1,419.4	MT3
10	Residual fuel oils	1,335.0	RB2

Source: United Nations Commodity Trade Statistics Database.
Note: HT1 = electronics and electrical products; MT3 = engineering products; RB2 = resource-based products.

Index

Figures, notes, and tables are indicated by f, n, and t following page numbers.

Lightning Source UK Ltd.
Milton Keynes UK
UKOW032001130213

206258UK00013B/650/P